RECIPES FOR LIFE

RECIPES FOR LIFE

My Memories

LINDA EVANS

with Sean Catherine Derek

Vanguard Press
A Member of the Perseus Books Group

Published by Vanguard Press
A Member of the Perseus Books Group

Cover photo courtesy John B. Cahoon III

Set in 11.5 point Adobe Garamond Pro

Cataloging-in-Publication data for this book is available from the Library of Congress.
ISBN 13: 978-1-59315-648-0

Vanguard Press books are available at special discounts for bulk purchases in the U.S. by corporations, institutions, and other organizations. For more information, please contact the Special Markets Department at the Perseus Books Group, 2300 Chestnut Street, Suite 200, Philadelphia, PA 19103, or call (800) 810-4145, ext. 5000, or e-mail special.markets@perseusbooks.com.

10 9 8 7 6 5 4 3 2 1

For Bunky, who has always been the wind at my back

Contents

CONTENTS

CONTENTS

LIST OF RECIPES

CONTENTS

Acknowledgments

MY SPECIAL THANKS to my stepdaughter, Sean, for her loving gift of helping me put my life into words.

Thank you to my dear friend Gary Craig, who inspired and encouraged me to weave my life and love of cooking together, which became the genesis of this book.

My brilliant young friend Laura Craig put the icing on the cake by tirelessly and miraculously collecting the many elements that it took to show the story of my life.

There are not enough words to thank my sister Charlie for helping me as she always has.

To my sister Kat and my brother-in-law Al: my heartfelt thanks for your love, support, recipe, and photos.

To Nena: thank you for being my kitchen companion all those years.

To Francine LaSala: thank you for the endless hours of help and creative joy.

Thank you to Nancy Langkopf and Kim Hanley, my ever-faithful friends and helpers, who wear so many hats so well.

I am so grateful to each and every one of these beautiful people for richly contributing to this book and my life:

Tracy Johansen, Peggy Ledyard, Johan Pool, Stephen Breimer, Tony Williams, John Cahoon, Alan Markfield, Gary Bernstein, Kari Mozena, Ann Limongello, JZ Knight, Dani Janssen, Anne Stewart, Pilar Wayne, Diana Welanetz Wentworth, Julia Child/Random House, Ina Garten/Random House, Nancy Baggett, Yuk Mai Leung Thayer, Linda McCallum, Luciana Paluzzi Solomon, Anda Allenson, Yorgo Chryssomallis, Stephen Atkinson, Bunny Stivers, Julie Heath, Mark Shepard, Jennifer

Hozer, Joel L. Bouvé, Dana Baker, Marlee Simmons, Gaye Ann Bruno, Carol Rosegg, Chris Nichols, Ashley James, David Bowers, Douglas Dubler, Barry King, Jerry Nagin, and Nolan Miller.

I also want to thank the Ronald Reagan Library, George Bush Presidential Library and Museum, ABC, ITV, Warner Bros. Entertainment Inc., CBS, Blue Angels, Circus of the Stars, NBC, Playboy, Universal Studios, Crown Copyright, and the Vatican.

And last, but certainly not least, thank you to Roger Cooper and Georgina Levitt and everyone at Vanguard Press for being a supportive family to me and making this dream come true.

GOUGERES

FROM PAGE 1

While it's perfectly acceptable to drop the dough by tablespoonfuls onto the baking sheet, a pastry bag fitted with an open tip gives you a little more consistency among the puffs, and simply is more fun, a pursuit that should always be encouraged.

Gougeres are best served warm, and are terrific with wine or champagne. You can serve them freshly baked, or make them in advance, freeze for up to a month, then reheat them directly from the freezer for about 5 minutes.

Piled in a basket or stacked in a pyramid, gougeres provide a warm and welcoming start to a wonderful evening.

GOUGERES

- 8 tablespoons (1 stick) unsalted butter
- 1 cup water
- 1/4 teaspoon salt
- 1 cup flour
- 4 eggs, beaten
- 1 cup finely grated Gruyere cheese, divided
- 2 teaspoons Dijon mustard or 1 teaspoon dry mustard
- 1/2 teaspoon freshly ground pepper

Preheat oven to 400 degrees. Line baking sheets with parchment paper.

Combine the butter, water and salt in a medium saucepan over low heat, stirring until the butter has melted. Bring mixture to a boil, then remove pan from the heat. Add the flour all at once and beat vigorously with a wooden spoon until the dough comes together in a mass. Return the pan to the stove and, over medium heat, continue to beat the dough for another minute until a thin film appears on the bottom of the pan.

Scrape the dough into the bowl of a stand mixer and beat on medium speed for 1 minute to cool it a bit. Before adding the beaten eggs, reserve about 1 tablespoon for the glaze.

Add the eggs in four increments, letting each addition be absorbed completely into the dough before adding the next. The mixture may look sloppy, but will magically come together in a very thick batter. (If you feel in need of a workout, you can beat in the eggs by hand.)

Add 3/4 cup of the cheese, reserving the rest for garnish. Beat in the cheese, mustard and pepper until well-blended.

Drop by tablespoonfuls onto parchment about 1 inch apart, or use a pastry bag to pipe 1-inch mounds onto the baking sheet. Using your fingertip or pastry brush, lightly coat the top of each puff with some of the reserved egg.

Bake for 20 minutes, then reduce heat to 350 degrees and bake for 10 to 15 minutes longer until they are golden brown. Immediately top each gougere with a few strands of the reserved cheese. Return the pans to the oven to "set" the cheese; it should take less than a minute. Serve warm.

To make ahead:

Gougeres can be baked, then frozen in plastic freezer bags for up to a month. When you're ready to reheat, place them frozen on the baking sheets at 325 degrees for 5 minutes.

Makes about 36 small puffs.

— Adapted from "The Art & Soul of Baking" from Sur La Table.

Chain Me to a Stove

FRIENDS LAUGH WHEN I tell them "You could chain me to a stove and I'd be happy." But it's the truth. My two favorite things in life are people and food. Combining them by preparing meals for the people I love is simply my recipe for joy.

My whole life I never could say no to food. I'm a mystery to my family. I was called "Bones" by my father when I was young and blessed

Victory in London.

with an incredible metabolism that allowed me to eat, eat, eat, with little consequences, and I still can. It has been one of the great pleasures of my life.

I started cooking when I was about twenty-three. It was rough going at the beginning, and then I discovered Julia Child's first cookbook, *Mastering the Art of French Cooking*. I was in heaven.

As I continued to experiment and learn and grow, I found it wasn't just the *cooking* I was deriving such pleasure from, it was also the *cooking for*. Finding the right menu for the right person was a wonderful experience, and when I hit it, the alchemy was delicious. Since the first time I cooked something special for someone and saw the joy it gave them, I've been hooked. It became my passion, though not my only passion.

Ironically, I never planned to become an actress. I'd always dreamed of having children, a loving husband, and a beautiful home. Destiny definitely took me down a less traditional road. I have had beautiful homes, and two marriages that started off very lovingly, and I've been a stepmother instead of a mom. Not exactly what I'd had in mind, but God knows I have no regrets. Life led me in directions I never imagined, but it has always fulfilled my heart's desire and has given me far more than I ever could have dreamed.

Acting has afforded me a lifetime of meeting remarkable people around the world. Sometimes I can't believe that I've actually dined with kings and queens and presidents, that I've been invited to everything from intimate dinners in quaint little villages to the most prestigious restaurants from Paris and Hong Kong to Sydney. I even spent my fortieth birthday in the dining car on the Orient Express en route to Venice.

From *Big Valley* to *Dynasty* and everything in between and since, I have been collecting recipes. Some are from world-renowned chefs, others were handed down through the generations. Some are from friends and celebrities I have known, and, of course, many are from the hundreds of cookbooks I have amassed over the last forty years.

I love experimenting: creating my own versions of recipes and testing them out on my friends. As I've said, one of the greatest gifts you can give to someone is to prepare their favorite meal. Being able to touch someone's heart, while doing something I adore, is one of the reasons I so love to cook.

Since those amazing *Dynasty* days, my life has continued to be a wondrous adventure, enabling me to travel the world, getting to know others and myself. I've learned so much more than just how to separate the yolk or all the lovely ways to set an inviting table. Certainly, my wild ride on *Hell's Kitchen* with Marco Pierre White was one of the greatest cooking experiences of my life. I've come to see the complete picture, why it's not just about preparing a meal, but the importance of friends gathering to share their hopes and dreams.

This book is a love letter to all those I have known and cherished and shared wonderful foods with. I hope that you will enjoy the people, the recipes, and the banquet that has been my life—so far.

Linda Evans

Hollywood Here We Come!

MY PARENTS WERE pretty typical of their generation: Mom cooked, Dad ate. My mother was one of those wonder cooks who could make gravy out of air and stretch a little pot of homemade soup to feed a small army, which she often did.

In 1943 my parents decided to move west. They had been working for years as professional ballroom dancers on the East Coast, but after my sister Carole (who is now known as Charlie) and I were born, my mother retired and we moved from Connecticut to California. My grandparents, Tony and Marie, were managers of a U-shaped complex in Hollywood and we moved into a charming little duplex right next to them. I loved it because it was on Sycamore Street, which actually was lined with beautiful old sycamore trees.

Daddy worked alone for a while, but then gave up dancing as well to become an interior wallpaper hanger / painter extraordinaire. He loved his job and would occasionally work in the homes of the famous, like Rudy Vallée and Dana Andrews.

It was tough work in those days. Daddy did not have paint rollers in 1948 or water-based paint and all the work was done with large, heavy brushes. Charlie and I always knew what color he was using since his white overalls would be splattered with the "Color of the Day."

My father truly loved everyone and "never met a stranger." Occasionally, he'd arrive home for dinner, walk in happy, and announce to Mom, "Add some water to the soup, honey, I've brought a new friend." While driving home, he'd see a homeless man sitting against a wall and invite him to dinner. Daddy would always make the "new friend" feel at home, offering him a drink and, of course, one of Mom's great meals. At the

1

Mom and Dad—my dancing stars.

end of the evening, he would get back in his car and drive many miles to return the man back to where he found him.

Each time it was a brand-new friend. It gave Daddy great joy to give some happiness to an individual—even if only for one night. We all loved him for this.

Incidentally, the only time Dad ever cooked for us was when we went to this little cabin in the forest. There were no modern conveniences, so Dad would just warm up a can of something or other on the wood-burning stove. But for a kid, that was more exciting than a fancy feast.

A Heart of Gold

WHEN I WAS around five and Charlie six, a mother and her little boy moved into an apartment in the back corner of our complex. The boy was very young, so my sister and I didn't play with him much. One day, there was a large banner across the little boy's door that read: ISOLATION POLIO–DO NOT ENTER. As a child it was hard for me to understand what was going on.

The little boy and his mother were quarantined, so she could not even leave to go to the store. The neighbors ignored them, but our

Daddy, Charlie, Mama, and me happy to be in Hollywood.

mother was far too compassionate to stand by and just watch them suffer. So, despite warnings, Mom would often cook meals for them and deliver them herself. In her heart, she believed she was safe and needed to do something to help.

Sadly, she was wrong. Polio was a rampant and deadly disease. Suddenly, our mother started complaining of severe aches in her body. The only thing that my grandfather could think to do was to put hot towels on her back directly from a large pot of boiling water. I can remember her crying out in pain because they were so hot. He did this several times a day. Later, the doctors said that this probably prevented her from having permanent paralysis.

Despite our grandfather's efforts, the next thing we knew an ambulance came and took our mother to the hospital. They said she had polio, but was very lucky in that it only affected her left shoulder and arm, and her right leg.

In the hospital, each day they would lower her into a pool, where, miraculously, she could move her arms and legs. She promised the nurses that she would do the Scottish hop (a dance step she knew, having been a professional dancer) down the hallway on the day she left.

While our mother was in the hospital, my sister and I were sent to separate homes to be taken care of. The families were strangers to us, but kind. Visiting days from Daddy were wonderful until he had to leave. Meanwhile, he was busy arranging for us to move into a new house in North Hollywood.

I remember the day my father, sister, and I moved into our first new home, and even though it was a small, two-bedroom in the Valley—with no lawn, just sand in front and back—we thought it was a palace.

A few months after we moved in, my mother was finally ready to leave the hospital. All the nurses, doctors, and interns lined the hallway and applauded her as she danced out the door. Thank God. Prayers are answered!

Our mother came home to our brand-new house. Needless to say it was quite a joyous occasion for all.

Bringing People Together

WHEN I BEGAN writing this book, I tried to remember when I first realized that even a modest, home-cooked meal can bring a person joy. One of my earliest memories of this is my mother's Hot Dog Stew.

It must have been around 1951, during the Korean War, because we often had a house full of servicemen to feed. A cousin on leave started bringing by a few of his buddies for dinner, which soon became a regular event at our house. Mom loved being able to do something special for these young men. Most were far from home and missing their own families. But we had very little money, so Mom cooked up her Hot Dog Stew.

The good old Hot Dog Stew days are the only entertaining I remember my family doing, besides Thanksgiving and Christmas. When I was fifteen, my dad passed away and my mother went on Social Security, so there would be no more parties. But the memories of how much everyone loved my mom for cooking for them is still fresh in my mind and heart.

MOM'S HOT DOG STEW

Like in most families, no one sees things the same way. Both my sister Charlie and I have our own versions of our mother's hot dog stew. And to keep peace in the family, I am sharing both versions with you.

MAKES 4 SERVINGS

---

2 tablespoons olive oil

1 pound hot dogs (preferably all pork), cut into 1½-inch slices at an angle

1 large green pepper, cut into 1½-inch pieces

1 large onion, cut into 1½-inch pieces

1 (16-ounce) can whole potatoes, drained and sliced ¼-inch thick

1 (28-ounce) can whole tomatoes

1 tablespoon dried oregano

1½ teaspoons garlic salt

Put the olive oil into a large Dutch oven or heavy casserole pan over medium-high heat. Add the hot dog pieces and cook, stirring often, about 6 minutes, until the skins are crispy and browned. Remove from the pan and set aside.

Put the pepper and onion in the oil remaining in the pan, and cook until the onions and peppers are translucent, about 6 minutes. Add the potatoes and cook until all the vegetables are lightly browned, about 6 more minutes.

Return the hot dogs to the pan. Pour the tomato juice from the can into the pan. Remove any cores or skin from the whole tomatoes, then pull them into pieces as you place them in the pan (your hands are the best tool for this job!). Sprinkle with oregano and garlic salt.

Simmer it slowly, covered, on top of the stove for 15 to 20 minutes.

Ladle it into bowls and serve with your favorite toasted garlic bread.

Here is what Charlie does differently:

Preheat the oven to 350°F.

Hold back the sliced potatoes until after the stew is cooked. Put the cold potatoes into the bottom of a large Pyrex baking dish and pour the stew (that has cooked for only 20 minutes) over the potatoes. Mix the potatoes into the stew, then generously sprinkle with Parmesan cheese. Charlie bakes it for 30 minutes and swears her version is better . . . sisters.

California Dreaming

MY OLDER SISTER Charlie and I are only eighteen months apart. She has always been strong-willed, extremely bright, and incredibly loving. To this day, Charlie is one of my closest and dearest friends. My younger sister, Kat (short for Kathy), was born a full decade after us. Despite the age difference, the three of us couldn't be closer.

Me, Charlie, and baby sister Kat make three.

When Charlie and I were kids, we held hands everywhere we went. Shy, I would always hide behind her when guests came to our house. She always took charge, especially over the tiny bedroom we shared, until she left at fifteen to marry her childhood sweetheart. Many times Charlie drew an imaginary line down the middle of the room to keep the peace. It worked. Today, she and I are neighbors on the same property in Washington State. Mama would be proud.

After we left Hollywood for North Hollywood, we didn't entertain as much. The long fold-up buffet table we'd used for Christmas and Thanksgivings sat in the garage collecting dust. That is, until one summer when I was nine, Charlie came up with a brilliant idea. We would put on a performance in our backyard.

We talked Mom into letting us use a beautiful blue velvet cape she wore from back when she and my father were professional ballroom dancers. We retrieved the cape from an old trunk, then we set the buffet table up as a stage in the yard, next to the garage. Charlie was to be the star, and she wore the cape for her performance. My job was to sit on the roof and sprinkle her with torn pieces of paper meant to look like snow while she sang "Winter Wonderland." All Charlie remembers of her first performance was my mom, rosary beads in her hand, praying that I didn't fall off the roof.

I guess you could say I started at the top.

Now, here we are. . . . All grown up.

Sweet Dancing Eyes

I HAVE SWEET memories of our family gathering for music nights with Mama, Daddy, Grandma, Grandpa, Charlie, and me. There were banjos, ukuleles, and singing. Charlie was an excellent singer. She got As in Glee Club, which obviously gave her the authority to announce to everyone, "Linda's off-key again!" And I was. Always. This is when I first learned to lip-sync, a talent that would later serve me well.

Sometimes during these evenings Mama and Daddy would play records from the 1940s and they would teach us dance steps like the tango, the cha-cha-cha, or the two-step.

I remember one time Mama got up at four in the morning to give me a waltz lesson for a part I was doing that day. I don't remember the project, just my mother's sweet dancing eyes as she led me around the living room floor. I wish those beautiful times could have lasted.

Sadly, the sweet memories became mixed with painful ones. My parents began having problems in their relationship and they both turned to alcohol to escape.

There was no way as I teenager I could see how this would later affect me and the choices I would make in my life. Unraveling these threads has been profoundly revealing. After their drinking started, life as we knew it began to dissolve.

When I was fifteen, both my parents became seriously ill and were hospitalized at the same time. My dad was diagnosed with inoperable cancer. There were no hospices in those days, so when they sent him home to die, Charlie moved back in with her husband, Art, to take care of him. Watching Daddy suffer and being powerless to stop it is one of the saddest and most painful times I have ever known in my life.

Mama had serious complications and the doctors said it was a miracle she survived. It was months before she came home from the hospital. Daddy died shortly after.

It took a long time, but some sweetness started to come back into our lives when our step-grandfather, Tony Vergoti, moved in with us after our grandmother passed away. He was the only grandfather we ever knew and we loved him dearly.

Grandpa Tony was also in show business, so to speak. He worked at Desilu Studios. One year, when I was in my early teens, he took me to the annual wrap party for *I Love Lucy,* which was being held at a little park near the studio.

At the end of the day, Lucy signed autographs. By the time I found out, I was at the back of an incredibly long line. It was getting late, so I was desperately hoping she wouldn't leave before I reached her. But even after dark, Lucy stayed on until she had given everyone, including me, her autograph. That experience meant so much that I've always tried to remember it anytime fans take the time to wait for me.

ONE OF MY FAVORITE PASTAS

Grandpa Tony had been a cook in the merchant marines and then later in New York, in small restaurants. It was heavenly to come home to the smell of garlic and tomatoes when he cooked for us. This recipe is a tribute to him.

MAKES 6 SERVINGS

1 pound penne pasta

3 tablespoons olive oil, divided

8 large Roma tomatoes, peeled and diced (page 56)

¼ pound large spinach leaves, washed, stems removed
    (I prefer prewashed leaves)

¼ cup (½ stick) unsalted butter, cut into small pieces

¾ teaspoon kosher salt

1 garlic clove, minced (or 1 to 2 more if you don't use the
    chili-garlic paste below)

1 pound raw large shrimp, shelled and cleaned, tails removed

1 tablespoon Chinese chili-garlic paste (I like Lan Chi brand), optional,
    to taste

Cook the penne according to manufacturer's directions.

While the pasta is boiling, heat 1 tablespoon of oil in a large saucepan over medium heat. Add the tomatoes and cook until the juice begins to run, about 5 minutes. Add the spinach and cook until slightly wilted. Turn heat to low and stir in butter, a piece at a time, until melted. Add the salt, then remove the pan from the heat, cover and keep warm.

Heat the remaining 2 tablespoons of oil in another skillet over medium heat. Add the garlic, sautéing until just lightly golden. Then add the shrimp and the chili paste, if using. Toss the shrimp to coat it in the sauce and sauté a few minutes, just until the shrimp turns pink and opaque. Remove from heat and add to the tomato-butter sauce.

In a large bowl combine the pasta and the tomato sauce and toss to coat. Divide the pasta among six plates, then spoon a portion of shrimp onto each plate.

Enjoy!

The Long Walk of Fame

EVEN AS A little girl, I believed in God, and more so, in the love of God. So it came as a shock when I heard one day in church that my Protestant girlfriend couldn't go to heaven because she wasn't Catholic. No part of my eight-year-old brain could comprehend how that could be true.

For a while, I stopped going to church, but I missed my connection with God. So I found a compromise: When I was fifteen, I worked as an usherette at the Paramount Theater in Hollywood, and I often spent my dinner hour in a nearby church around the corner. No service. No people. No words. Just God and me, hanging out together. I realize now that it was the beginning of a spiritual quest that would become the greatest journey of my life, one that would actually take me back along the path where my spiritual journey had started. Years later, surrounded by family and friends, I was presented with my own star on the Hollywood Walk of Fame—in front of the Paramount Theater.

Ursula and John help this usherette celebrate her star.

PEACH HEAVEN

I always look forward to summer because I can make this amazing dish with fresh peaches. As a sweet tribute to my spiritual journey and the "heaven" I was in when I earned my star, here's one of my favorite desserts.

Although the instructions call for broiling the sugar topping, this is the ideal recipe for using a crème brûlée torch if you have one!

16

MAKES 4 TO 6 SERVINGS

2 pounds peaches

1½ cups whipping cream

1½ tablespoons vanilla extract

1½ cups dark brown sugar (or more as needed)

Bring a large pot of water to the boil. Working in batches, drop the peaches in the boiling water and blanch for about 60 seconds (the skin on a super-ripe peach may burst in as little as 30 seconds, so watch them). Use a slotted spoon to transfer the peaches to a bowl of ice water. Remove the skins, which will now slip off easily under your fingers. Slice the peaches into ½-inch segments and arrange them in an 11 x 8-inch ovenproof dish (they should go about halfway up the sides of the dish).

Beat the cream and vanilla with an electric mixer on high until soft peaks form. (If it's a warm day, it speeds the whipping to chill the empty bowl and the metal beaters in the freezer for a few minutes before starting.) Spread the cream over the peaches and freeze for 2 hours. (Do not freeze for longer than 2 hours, because the peaches will be too frozen to serve right away.)

To serve, preheat the broiler.

Take the dish out of the freezer and sprinkle the brown sugar on the top, coating the entire surface of the cream heavily with sugar, about ¼-inch thick. (I press the brown sugar through a sieve to remove any lumps and allow it to sprinkle more evenly.) If you need a little more sugar to cover the entire surface of the cream, or if your peaches aren't at the height of summer sweetness, feel free to add a little more sugar.

Place the dish under the broiler and broil about 4 minutes. Watch it constantly because it can burn very easily. You may need to turn your pan so it cooks evenly. When the sugar has melted and just starts to bubble, and when the cream starts showing through, it's done. Serve at once.

Out of My League

THE FIRST TRULY elegant dinner I ever attended was when I was sixteen. I was dating a young man named William Keck. His family was in "oil." He invited me over to dinner to meet his parents, and on the menu that night was an amazing beef dish, a meal that I, growing up on limited funds, had never had. But that wasn't going to be all that was different about dining with this family and mine.

I never knew people needed more than one fork, knife, and spoon to eat. The table was set with—what seemed to me at the time—dozens of each, and all gold. If that wasn't intimidating enough, when the butler brought the tray over to me, I didn't know how to use the serving pieces to get the food onto my plate.

There I was, horrified, not realizing *yet* that every nightmare has a blessing. There are no mistakes in the universe! Years later, when I was playing Krystle Carrington on *Dynasty*, it was easy for me to relate to Krystle's discomfort trying to adjust to the "rich life." Now that I think of it, I may owe the Kecks for my Golden Globe Award.

Dragged into Destiny

MY MOTHER WASN'T really surprised when my junior high school English teacher told her I was so shy that I wouldn't get up in class to give my book report, and that it was time I overcame it. Her suggestion: Take drama class or flunk English. Sometimes you are dragged into destiny.

The family joke is that my first acting part was Sleeping Beauty, a break for me since I slept through most of the play. Somehow I survived junior high drama class, but I still didn't like getting up in front of people.

When I was fifteen and in high school, my friend Carol Wells asked me to keep her company while she waited to audition for a national commercial. Carol had already done a number of commercials, so she knew how long these "cattle calls" could take.

When we arrived, there were over fifty girls waiting to interview and we ended up waiting for hours. Finally, when there were only six girls left in the room, the director came out and pointed at me, telling me to come in.

Confused, I said, "I'm just here visiting with my friend."

Carol was then invited in. When she came out, she said, "He wants you."

Reluctantly I went in and the director told me he wanted me for the commercial. I tried to explain that I wasn't an actress.

"Can you sit on a carousel, next to a boy, and drink a bottle of ginger ale?" he asked.

"Of course," I said. "But I would never do that to my friend."

He promised me that if I accepted the part he would give Carol another commercial. In a town of broken promises, he kept his word. His name was Gerald Schnitzer. Not only did he give my girlfriend the part he'd promised, he gave me several more. Even though I was scared to death, I knew I had to accept this amazing gift (with Carol's blessing and encouragement), especially as it would allow me to contribute and help ease the tight budget we were on at home. I didn't understand at the time the magic life was weaving for me.

MOM'S BAKED MAC AND CHEESE

If there's one thing all three of us girls remember it's Mom's macaroni and cheese. What we don't remember is exactly how she made it, and we all have our variations on it. I like it with sharp cheddar, Charlie with medium.

MAKES 8 TO 10 SERVINGS

1½ pounds large elbow macaroni
2¼ pounds cheddar cheese, grated
5 ounces (1¼ sticks) unsalted butter, cut into small cubes
Salt and freshly ground pepper, to taste
3 cups whole milk

Preheat oven to 350°F.

Cook macaroni in a pot of boiling salted water, until tender but still firm to the bite. Drain and rinse with cold water. Place half of the cooled macaroni in a 15½ x 10½-inch baking dish. Cover with half the cheese, and dot with half the butter. Salt and pepper the entire layer and repeat. Again, the cheese should cover the macaroni completely—even the corners.

On the stovetop, heat milk to scalding hot, but not boiling. Slowly pour over the mac and cheese combination.

Bake for 45 minutes to 1 hour, until all the milk is absorbed. (I place a sheet of foil on the bottom of the oven in case the milk boils over in the oven.) Serve warm.

Note: This recipe makes a lot but leftovers freeze well. Leftovers can be cut into squares sized to individual portions and stored in freezer bags.

My Magical MGM Days

LOOKING BACK I realize how incredibly fortunate I was to have been one of the last contract players at one of the most historically rich studios: MGM. However, like so many things in life that end wonderfully, the road leading there was seriously bumpy.

I'd been working intermittently, doing small parts, since I was fifteen, so at nineteen, I was thrilled to land the lead in a pilot called *Buttons*. The hairdresser decided my dishwater blonde hair needed to be darker and that I'd look better with a permanent. Trusting that a professional would know what was best for me, I, of course, was shocked and horrified that night, when half my hair was clogging the shower drain. I ended up wearing a Debbie Reynolds–style red wig and the pilot was never picked up.

What appeared to be a disaster was an incredible opportunity. MGM decided to put me under contract around that time and sent me to Sidney Guileroff, who was one of the top hair stylists in Hollywood. Sidney changed my life forever, by making me a blonde.

My first movie, *Twilight of Honor*, was with Richard Chamberlain. (Richard and I dated off and on over the years. I also guest-starred on *Dr. Kildare*.) In the film, I played a young girl who had just lost her father. In my only scene in the film, I had to throw myself onto the casket as it was being lowered into the ground and sob. We shot the burial scene from many different angles all day.

I remember thinking that acting was going to be tougher than I thought. This was not something my high school drama class had prepared me for. The good news was that MGM had a wonderful drama coach! I trusted Vincent Chase completely, and he really understood

22

me and my fear of getting up in front of people and performing. We had quite a laugh forty-five years later when he surprised me in Los Angeles by coming to see *Legends*, the play I was starring in with Joan Collins. Certainly it was not a moment Vincent or I would have bet on.

Being at MGM was amazing. I also studied with Gertrude Fogler, a diction coach, in a little cottage on the lot. All the young stars of the thirties and forties, like Judy Garland and Mickey Rooney, had studied there with her. She had me read *The Little Prince* in French to slow me down because the studio said I spoke too fast.

During those magical days I spent on the lot, you could still see some of the greatest stars of all time and watch them on the set. In fact, the very first time I ever saw Barbara Stanwyck, she was filming with Elvis Presley. At the time, I never imagined I would soon be working with her and that she would become so very important in my life.

From Bikinis to Boots

SHORTLY AFTER FILMING *Beach Blanket Bingo*, my agent sent me to audition for a movie called *The Glory Guys*. It was being produced by Levy-Gardner-Laven, so I was very excited. I remember thinking how great it would be to get another movie. Two in a row—I'd look like a real professional!

The director, Arnold Laven, invited me in to read for the part. When I finished, he just stared at me in silence. "That was the worse reading I've ever heard," he said.

So much for looking like a professional. I wanted to get out of there as fast as I could, so I sheepishly thanked him and started for the door.

Sugar Kane was my name, and singing was NOT my game.

But he stopped me before I could escape. "We're doing another project and I think you have the right qualities for it," he told me.

The other project was *The Big Valley*—thank God for second chances.

I still had to test for the role of Audra, the daughter of Victoria Barkley, who would be played by Barbara Stanwyck. It came down to three actresses. Ironically, I was paired with a young man that I'd met a year before at a friend's home, the very first day he'd arrived in Los Angeles with his wife and baby. We ended up doing the screen test together and were thrilled that we both got hired. His name was Lee Majors.

Lee and Me.

Marjoram, Missy, and Thyme

I'VE HAD THE privilege of meeting a lot of celebrities. I was even part of the remarkable *Night of a Hundred Stars*. But few in Hollywood history were bigger or brighter than Barbara Stanwyck, known as Missy to her friends and crew.

She was one of a kind—tiny but mighty. She believed in having protein for breakfast, preferably steak. When she decided I needed more energy, she'd order a steak for me, too. If that failed to get me moving fast enough, Missy would have us hop on our bikes and ride over to the studio doctor to get vitamin B12 shots, which usually happened at least twice a week.

One day Missy burst into my dressing room and, in that powerful manner she was so famous for, said, "Audra, I am going to teach you how to be in this business. You've got to do two things, show up on time and know your lines." She took me under her wing and became my guiding light for many years.

Aside from the obvious gifts Missy gave me, I also got so much from just watching her. She was as respected within Hollywood for her outstanding work ethic as for her incredible talent. She set the example that I have lived by and I know for a fact that I was often hired simply because producers knew they could count on me. One of the best examples of this was when Kenny Rogers was looking for a costar for the *Gambler* sequel. He told my agent that he would only work with someone known to be very professional . . . which must have been true, since you better believe I didn't get the part for my singing talent!

It was Missy who taught me it was okay, even fun, to do my own stunts. I remember the first time the director approached me on *The Big*

Mom and the kids.

Valley to ask me if I would mind not using my stunt double for an up-coming scene because Missy was going to do it herself. If neither of us used a double, they could film us closer and make it much more exciting. I didn't even question what the stunt would be—I just figured if Missy was doing it, it couldn't be *too* dangerous. (I later learned that she did a film called *Forty Guns* where she was thrown from her horse, with her foot caught in a stirrup, and dragged. There's no actress, before or since, who has been filmed doing this stunt. God I loved this woman!)

Missy and I always made sure we had our own stuntwomen on the set and that they were paid whether they worked or not. Obviously I would never have dared to do anything that required great skill. Throughout my career, I have watched the talented stuntmen and stuntwomen in awe. But like Missy, I became passionate about doing them, and when a new script would come in, we'd huddle together to see if we'd get to escape a burning building or battle our way through a band of bad guys. After that first stunt together, Missy and I did as many as we could. It was just one more thing we enjoyed doing together and it brought us even closer.

I was so fortunate to have been working with such a legend. Once, during a scene in which Missy and I had to enter a room together, the director felt I just wasn't getting it. After several takes, Missy pulled me aside and said, "Audra, come into the room with *presence*." After a few more takes, the director still wasn't happy, but he was ready to move on. Missy said, "Virgil, let's try it one more time."

The camera rolled, the director called "Action!" and I opened the door and started into the room. Then Missy gave me a swift kick in the butt, propelling me ahead of her with such force that I delivered my lines with a sudden vitality. As if she hadn't just booted me, Missy entered and said her lines with her usual perfection. The director happily yelled, "Cut! Print!"

Missy turned to me and said, "That's what I mean by presence."

MISSY'S HOBO FILLET

During the four years we filmed *The Big Valley*, Missy introduced me to her favorite restaurant, the famous Chasen's. She loved their Hobo Steak. We continued having dinner there even while I was doing *Dynasty*, which is when I created my own twist on this classic steak recipe: using filet mignon rather than their more traditional New York strip steak.

MAKES 4 SERVINGS

6 ounces (1½ sticks) unsalted butter

2 teaspoons dried marjoram

1 teaspoon dried rosemary

½ teaspoon dried thyme

Salt, to taste

2 pounds filet mignon, sliced ½-inch thick

8 to 12 slices sourdough bread, about 3 inches across and ¼-inch thick

Clarify the butter by heating it in a heavy-bottomed saucepan over low heat until the butter starts to foam. Remove the pan from the heat and skim the foam and any solids off the top. Pour the butter into a glass measuring cup, which makes it easier to see the pure yellow fat floating on top of the milky liquid. Use a small ladle or spoon to lift the clarified butter off the milky liquid.

Mix together the dried herbs and lightly sprinkle a little of the mixture and a little salt over one side of the fillet. Heat about ¼ cup of the clarified butter in a large skillet on medium-high heat. Put the sliced fillet herb-side-down in the skillet and then sprinkle a little more of the herb mixture and salt over it. For rare, cook each side about 1 to 2 minutes just to brown the outside, or cook to your preference. Place the fillet on a holding plate.

Add more clarified butter and a few herbs into the same skillet. Working in batches, put the bread slices into the skillet and toast. Flip the bread to brown the other side, adding additional butter and herbs. Continue until all the bread is toasted golden brown.

Divide the toasts among four serving plates. Take the fillet slices from the holding plate and place the meat on top of the toast. Pour any of the meat juice that accumulated on the holding plate over the meat and toast and enjoy.

Like a Second Mother

FROM THE FIRST day I met Barbara Stanwyck, she called me "Audra" (my character's name) and became like a second mother to me. When my own mother passed away during *The Big Valley* years, Missy told me, "I know I can never replace your mother, but I'll be your mom now." Then she wrapped her arms around me and held me tight.

Missy was a remarkable lady and an incredibly loyal friend. One year she told the producers that she would not return to work unless they agreed to build me a private bathroom in my dressing room next to hers.

She was always very protective of me, too. When *TV Guide* sent a reporter to interview me for a possible cover story, Missy spent a long time talking to him about me. He spent days on the set interviewing the cast and even the crew. Everyone was very pleased when my picture appeared on the cover. But Missy was not pleased with the lead-in: "Will anyone remember Linda Evans in twenty years?"

Ironically, twenty years later, Missy and I were having dinner together, celebrating my success on *Dynasty*, when a very elegant lady approached our table and said to me: "You cannot continue letting your husband's staff treat you that way. You must take control of your house. Believe me, I know these things." Then she flipped her fur over her shoulder and walked away, leaving me staring in disbelief. Missy turned to me and said: "Well, dear, it would seem your show is a success, since she obviously wasn't drunk, but still thinks you're Krystle. Isn't that funny, Audra?"

Missy was always looking out for me. *The Big Valley* had a limited budget for Audra's wardrobe. But Missy went to the producers and told

31

Missy and me together again on Dynasty.

them that her daughter needed more clothes. When they said they couldn't afford it, Missy asked, "Isn't Victoria Barkley rich?"

Apparently, Victoria was rich enough only for her to have an extensive wardrobe. So Missy asked Nolan Miller (our wonderful costume designer) to take some of her dresses from previous episodes and alter them to fit me—no easy task since I was a least four inches taller and my shoulders even wider. But somehow, Nolan managed to make it work. (Years later, on *Dynasty*, Nolan was so happy that he could "set my broad shoulders free" and helped create an entire new era of beautifully designed clothes with shoulder pads.)

My Dream Man

LONG BEFORE I ever met actor John Derek, I was in love with him. When I was twelve, I saw the movie *The Adventures of Hajji Baba*, which I thought was incredibly romantic, with a turbaned John riding across the sand dunes on an Arabian horse. I immediately got the record of Nat King Cole singing the title song and listened to it over and over (until my sister Charlie wanted to kill me).

Like so many teenagers at that time, I had a picture of John over my bed (next to Tab Hunter) and I spent many hours staring into his beautiful eyes. I remember being heartsick when I read in a movie magazine that he was married with two children.

The first time I met John was years later, when he had become a filmmaker/photographer. He'd seen the pilot for *The Big Valley* and called the producers to ask if he could photograph me. Of course I said yes. He had a reputation of being an exceptional photographer. By this time he had divorced his first wife and was now married to Ursula Andress.

I was delighted to discover that he was as handsome and charming as I'd imagined. He was also incredibly romantic, referring to Ursula as his bride after nine years of marriage. His home looked like it was right out of *Hajji Baba*. He'd handmade much of the furniture, which was covered in silks and furs, and there were candles everywhere. He even created a huge waterfall that cascaded down his Encino hillside, which could be seen through huge walls of glass in all the rooms.

We spent the whole day shooting pictures. I didn't think about it again until many months later, when he called and asked if I'd like to see the pictures and maybe even take a few more.

This time when I got to his house, I learned that Ursula had left John, staying in France with her costar, Jean-Paul Belmondo. That was the beginning of our wondrously romantic relationship. I was so in love that when John suggested that I try to get out of doing *The Big Valley*, I wholeheartedly agreed. However, the producers thought it was a really bad idea. We compromised and I did a few less episodes a season, which is why Audra was often "off in Stockton shopping."

Many nights after I'd been filming *The Big Valley*, I'd come home to find a house totally dark except for a roaring fire and candles twinkling from every corner. I was amazed how much thought John put into making me feel loved, as if I was the most important person in the world. Some nights as I was walking in, he'd hand me a huge antique silver goblet filled with sparkling wine and fresh strawberries.

Frank Edwards © Fotos International

A rare night out.

Other nights he'd hand-dip grapes in egg white and dust them with powdered sugar, then feed them to me one by one in front of the fire.

Years later, when I was "married" to my "other John"—John Forsythe—on *Dynasty*, I told him about those romantic nights and he mentioned it to the producers, who decided to incorporate it into the show. Every time Blake and Krystle did one of those scenes, John Forsythe would teasingly ask me if it was as romantic as it was with "my first John."

John and I never planned to get married. He had told me over and over that he never wanted to get married again, and I was happy just being with him. It was something that really happened on the spur of the moment. We literally woke up one morning, and he turned to me and said we should get married. That day. So off we drove to Mexico, with John's daughter Sean in tow as a witness. He wore off-white jeans and I wore white ones.

My Favorite Mexican Recipes

John and I got married in Mexico. Everything happened so fast, we barely had time to eat, which was really a shame because we both loved Mexican food. Here are some of my favorite recipes collected through the years. The first three were taught to me when I was married to John by my first cooking teacher, Diana Welanetz Wentworth, who has several wonderful cookbooks that I still use. And the last one, the Fish Tacos, is from my good friend Linda McCallum. To this day, the chicken and cheese enchiladas are my all time favorite. Sometimes I make them with just cheese.

CHICKEN AND CHEESE ENCHILADAS

MAKES 12 ENCHILADAS

BASIC ENCHILADA SAUCE

4 ounces (1 stick) unsalted butter

½ cup all-purpose flour

2 (19-ounce) cans mild red chile enchilada sauce (I like Las Palmas)

3 cups chicken broth

¼ teaspoon oregano

¼ teaspoon ground cumin

1 chicken bouillon cube

1 pound cooked chicken (rotisserie chicken from the supermarket
   works well)

1 pound Monterey Jack cheese, coarsely grated

2 bunches scallions (including some of the green tops), sliced, divided

Vegetable oil

12 corn tortillas

1 (16-ounce) container sour cream

First make the enchilada sauce. Melt the butter in a heavy-bottomed
skillet. Stir in the flour and cook over very low heat for 3 to 4 minutes,
stirring. This cooking of the roux prevents the sauce from having a raw,
floury taste. Do not allow the flour to burn, though it is all right if it
colors slightly. Remove the pan from the heat and let cool for a minute
or so. Stir in the enchilada sauce and the chicken broth. Return the pan
to the heat and bring the sauce to a simmer while stirring with a wire
whisk. Add the herbs and chicken bouillon and let simmer over very low
heat for 10 minutes, stirring often. If the sauce seems thin, continue
simmering a few minutes longer. Set aside, covered.

Make the filling by shredding the one pound of meat from the rotisserie chicken into bite-size pieces, then combining it in a mixing bowl with the Monterey Jack cheese and half the scallions. Mix well to blend.

Preheat oven to 350°F.

Heat ⅛ inch of oil over medium heat in a small skillet. Dip one tortilla at a time into the hot oil for a few seconds to soften it. Remove and put on a plate with paper towels; pat dry and set aside. Continue with the rest of the tortillas, adding more oil as needed.

On another plate, place a scant amount of enchilada sauce and some of the filling mixture in the center of each tortilla and roll it up securely. Place the rolls, seam side down, in a 13 x 9-inch baking and serving dish, taking care that they are at least ¾ inch apart.

Just before baking, reheat the remaining enchilada sauce and pour it evenly over the top of the enchiladas. Bake for 15 to 20 minutes, or until the cheese is melted and the sauce is sizzling around the edges of the pan. Before serving, top each enchilada with a large dollop of sour cream and a sprinkling of the remaining sliced scallions.

PUERCO PICANTE

If you don't think you are a pork lover, you will be after this!

MAKES 12 SERVINGS

7 pounds lean pork shoulder roast, boneless

1 teaspoon salt

2 tablespoons commercial mixed pickling spices

1 tablespoon whole cumin seeds, or ground cumin

1 teaspoon whole black peppercorns

1 teaspoon dried oregano

5 cloves garlic, pressed

2 tablespoons dark-red chili powder

3 to 4 tablespoons Mexican chili powder

3 (8-ounce) cans tomato sauce

2 tablespoons (¼ stick) unsalted butter

1 large onion, finely diced

2 cups canned chicken broth (or more)

Trim all fat from the pork and cut the meat into 1-inch cubes.

Using an electric blender, grind together the salt, pickling spices, cumin, peppercorns, and oregano. Place these spices in a mixing bowl with the garlic, chili powders, and tomato sauce. Cover the bowl and set the mixture aside.

Melt the butter in a large pot over medium heat. Add the meat and brown very slowly, stirring it occasionally, until most of the liquid the meat gives off has evaporated—this will take about an hour. Add the onion and sauté until transparent. Stir in the sauce mixture and chicken broth and simmer for about 2 hours, until the meat is tender. If the sauce becomes too thick, add a little more chicken broth.

To make ahead: The flavor will improve greatly if the pork is made ahead and either refrigerated or frozen, then reheated to serve. Reheat at 350°F, covered, for about 30 minutes or until thoroughly heated.

Serve with white rice, buttered noodles, or Rice Casserole with Sour Cream, Cheese, and Chiles (page 40). It's rich but worth it!

RICE CASSEROLE WITH
SOUR CREAM, CHEESE, AND CHILES

MAKES AT LEAST 10 SERVINGS

6 cups cooked white or brown rice (page 41)

3 cups sour cream, divided

Salt and pepper

1 (4-ounce) can diced green chiles, divided

1 pound Monterey Jack cheese, coarsely grated, divided

8 scallions (including some of the green tops), chopped, divided

Cheddar cheese, grated, for the topping

Preheat oven to 350°F. Grease a 4-quart ovenproof serving dish.

Place one-third of the cooked rice in the prepared dish. Evenly dot 1 cup of the sour cream over the rice and sprinkle generously with salt and pepper. Sprinkle with half of the chiles, half of the Monterey Jack cheese, and half of the chopped scallions. Repeat all of the layers, in the same order. Top with the last third of the rice and the sour cream. Sprinkle with salt and pepper and top with grated cheddar cheese.

Bake for about 20 minutes, or until the cheese is melted and the rice heated all the way through.

To make ahead: The casserole may be stored, baked or unbaked, in the refrigerator for 3 days.

WHITE RICE

2 cups water

½ teaspoon salt, or to taste

1 teaspoon vegetable oil or butter

1 cup white long-grain rice

In a medium-sized saucepan, bring the water, salt, and olive oil to a boil. Add the rice and give it a quick stir. Reduce heat to medium-low and cover. Simmer for 20 minutes. Then, keeping covered, remove from heat and let rest for 5 minutes.

Remove the lid and fluff with a fork. Serve immediately or keep warm.

TIPS:

Do not remove the lid while cooking rice. The steam is what actually cooks the rice.

You may find it helpful near the end of the 20 minutes cooking time to peek under the lid briefly. You can then see if the rice needs a little more water. You may add water but do not stir. If it is too moist, uncover it and cook a few more minutes.

Always fluff with a fork before serving.

FISH TACOS WITH GARLIC AÏOLI SAUCE

This is my favorite fish taco recipe. I make my fish tacos on flour tortillas but feel free to use corn tortillas if you prefer.

MAKES 6 SERVINGS

FOR THE AÏOLI:

2 tablespoons extra-virgin olive oil

6 large or 8 medium garlic cloves, minced

1 cup mayonnaise

½ teaspoon lime juice, or more to taste

Salt and lemon pepper

FOR THE FISH:

2 pounds firm, meaty fish fillets, such as halibut, cod, or salmon

3 tablespoons extra-virgin olive oil

1 teaspoon unsalted butter

Salt and lemon pepper, to taste

1 small lime, or to taste

FOR THE TORTILLAS:

Cooking spray

12 flour tortillas

4 ounces cheddar cheese, grated (about 1 cup)

FOR THE CONDIMENTS:

8 scallions (the white and barely green parts only), chopped

½ cup chopped cilantro

2 avocados, sliced (or 1 cup of your favorite guacamole)

2 large tomatoes, chopped

2 to 3 cups thinly sliced white cabbage (about ¼ of a large head)

Hot sauce

Salsa

FOR THE AÏOLI:

Heat the olive oil in a heavy skillet over medium heat for 1 to 2 minutes, then add the garlic and cook until just golden brown. Stir the garlic into the mayonnaise along with the lime juice, and add salt and lemon pepper to taste. Set aside.

FOR THE FISH:

Pat the fish dry with paper towels. (Removing as much liquid as possible from the surface allows the edges to turn gold and crisp up more readily.)

Place a heavy nonstick skillet over medium heat and add 1½ tablespoons olive oil and ½ teaspoon of butter (the butter flavors the oil). When the butter is melted, lay in half of the fillets. Cook, turning once, until the fish is cooked through and the edges are golden. The cooking time will vary according to the thickness of the fish, but thin fillets take 2 to 3 minutes per side and thicker fillets usually take about 5 to 6 minutes per side. The fish should still be slightly translucent in the center when done and easily flake when separated with a fork.

When the fish is done, move to a serving plate and season with salt, lemon pepper, and the juice from half a lime. Keep the cooked fish warm while you repeat this cooking process with the remaining fish.

FOR THE TORTILLAS:

Spritz the cooking spray into the bottom of a heavy skillet over medium heat. Add a tortilla, and when it's warm on one side, flip it, and add a sprinkling of cheddar cheese to taste. When the cheese melts remove the tortilla. Repeat this process until six of the twelve tortillas have been used.

Put the prepared tortillas on individual plates. Divide half the fish among the six tortillas and serve to your guests, who should add condiments to taste. Meanwhile, prepare the remaining tortillas, dividing the remaining fish among them, and serve.

An Unusual Recipe for Friendship

I REMEMBER BEING incredibly anxious when John said he wanted me to meet his good friends Carl and Bunky Vernell. I knew that Bunky was still best friends with Ursula. Although Ursula left John for French star Jean-Paul Belmondo, many believed she would one day try and get him back.

So what were the odds Bunky and I would become friends?

The dreaded day finally came to have dinner at their house in Encino. Bunky answered the door and much to my surprise, as I looked into her eyes, I just loved her. To this day, she has remained my oldest and dearest friend.

Meet my outrageous friend, Bunky.

That first night, I also met Bunky's family: her eldest, Michael, who was thirteen, the twins, Chris and Kelly, who were six, and her little girl Tracy, who was eight (and who, some forty years later, became my personal assistant while I toured with the play *Legends*).

When it came time for dinner, Bunky brought out her meatloaf and my jaw dropped, along with John's. It was shaped like a massive phallus, complete with meat "balls" and parsley.

Bunky's kids just looked at each other and rolled their eyes. "Oh, Mom. Not meatloaf again!" Evidently, they had seen all this before.

I soon learned that the reason Bunky was so "inventive" with her meatloaf was because she was bored, a state I have learned brings out the most outrageous in her. She had had a couple of glasses of wine, became inspired by the great sculptor Rodin, and began sculpting her masterpiece.

We spent many fabulous evenings at Bunky's home and I discovered that her husband Carl was also a great cook. Wanting to reciprocate, I decided to take cooking lessons for the first time.

My Béarnaise Fiasco
or Meltdown Washout

SEAN WAS AS excited about my becoming her new stepmother as I was. She was one of the best things to come out of my marriage to John, and certainly the most lasting.

When John and I first got together, his two children were living in Europe with their mother, Pati, a French prima ballerina and the grand niece of Leo Tolstoy. When I read about her in movie magazines when I was a kid, I thought she sounded really impressive—and in actuality, she was. We ended up being great friends.

Sean and I had already been pen pals, so when they got back to the states, we were both excited about meeting in person. Since that day, forty-plus years ago, we've remained very close friends and family. She even has her summerhouse next to mine in Washington State.

Sean came into my life right at the time I began pursuing two of my greatest passions: cooking and spirituality. John had no interest in either of these, but he appreciated my spending time with his daughter, who luckily showed an interest in both. So Sean became my spiritual sidekick, kitchen helper, and new-recipe taster (not always the best job in those early days). She was also witness to my first cooking disaster.

John had invited a group of his favorite friends for dinner. He would be cooking on his unique barbecue, which he built himself out of a single piece of volcanic rock. Another thing he handmade was our enormous tablecloth, which he created using longhair French cowhides. It was great for repelling spilled wine, but it was a bit strange washing my tablecloth with shampoo. But then, John was eccentric. John was also a red-meat-only man, so he would grill an entire uncut filet mignon,

John and his prima wife, Pati.

which he injected with red vermouth and herbs and coated with honey to keep in the juices.

I painstakingly prepared my first béarnaise sauce, which I had learned from Julia Child's *Mastering the Art of French Cooking*. To my relief, it turned out beautifully. A few minutes before the meat was ready, I put warm water into the kitchen sink, then carefully set my bowl of béarnaise into it to keep it warm. Then I went to get everything else ready.

I returned a few minutes later to find my perfect béarnaise swimming in water. To my horror, the faucet had leaked. The sauce was reduced to liquid, and I to tears.

Cooking lesson number one: Never define yourself or your value by whether you burn the buns or swamp the sauce. I was the only one who thought I'd ruined the evening. Cooking and everything else became a lot more fun when I stopped being so hard on myself—but that was a lesson that took a long time coming.

JULIA'S BÉARNAISE

Like any recipe you prepare over and over again, you begin to put your own twist on things. Perhaps one chef you admire uses too much garlic for your taste, or you might like someone's version of a cream sauce, but there may be an element someone else uses that you like even better. So you mix and match and you make it your own. But in Julia's case, she made the definitive béarnaise sauce. Here's Julia's original béarnaise (reprinted with permission from *Mastering the Art of French Cooking*)—I hope you like it as much as I do!

FOR 1½ CUPS

¼ cup wine vinegar

¼ cup dry white wine or dry white vermouth

1 Tb minced shallots or green onions

1 Tb minced fresh tarragon or ½ Tb dried tarragon

⅛ tsp pepper

Pinch of salt

A small saucepan

3 egg yolks

2 Tb cold butter

½ to ⅔ cup melted butter

2 Tb fresh minced tarragon or parsley

Boil the vinegar, wine, shallots or onions, herbs, and seasonings over moderate heat until the liquid has reduced to 2 tablespoons. Let it cool.

Then proceed as though making a hollandaise. Julia's hollandaise sauce, which I think is perfect, is also included in this book for you (page 80). Beat the egg yolks until thick. Strain in the vinegar mixture and beat. Add 1 tablespoon of cold butter and thicken the egg yolks over low heat. Beat in the other tablespoon of cold butter, then the melted butter by droplets. Correct seasoning, and beat in the tarragon or parsley.

European Excursions

BEFORE JOHN AND I fell in love, I'd never been out of the United States. John was thrilled, since he liked being the first to show me beautiful new places. He felt the best way to do it was by car, so we bought a silver-gray Jaguar in Zurich, Switzerland, and drove straight to Bern to see Ursula's family. We even went hiking in the mountains with Urs's amazing mom, who, in her late eighties, could still leave us behind.

John wanted to head north, do a tour of the Baltic countries, and show me my roots in Norway. But all I could think of was that I was so close to the place I had dreamed of all my life: France.

The moment we drove across the Swiss border and our tires touched French soil, John said I cried for two hours; I was so excited. I've always had an inexplicable love and passion for France. The day I went to Versailles, I felt like I had gone home. Even when I was in junior high and high school in Southern California, I took French instead of the more customary Spanish. Later I went to Berlitz and took so many French lessons that my teacher, André Demir, ended up being one of John's best friends.

My connection to France is wondrous; my love of French cooking, and that thread that has gone throughout my life in so many ways.

John and I did end up driving all around Europe, including seeing my ancestor's homeland, Norway.

Always a Great Notion

JOHN ALSO INTRODUCED me to camping. One summer, we traveled the entire California coast, then made our way up to Oregon to visit two of his closest friends on location. Richard Jaeckel and Sam Gilman had both landed roles in *Sometimes a Great Notion,* a film based on a best seller, starring Paul Newman. John had worked with Paul on *Exodus,* so he felt comfortable visiting them all.

It was a wonderful experience for everyone. I also had the honor of meeting Paul's wife, Joanne Woodward. I loved that they were living proof that a Hollywood marriage could work.

One of the first photos John took of me.

Paul wasn't only starring in *Sometimes a Great Notion*, he was also directing it—and so well that the film earned Richard Jaeckel an Oscar nomination.

Paul and I crossed paths again when I was doing the play *Legends* and he agreed to play the voice of Paul Newman, as it had been written years before when Carol Channing and Mary Martin were the stars. Paul made a recording for the show, and it was great fun hearing his voice every night for nine months while we did the play.

For our next camping trip, John bought an Excalibur, which was styled after the 1928 Mercedes-Benz S convertible tourer. John not only loved driving that car but at night he used it to create these wonderful *Hajji Baba*–style tents for us; each time, making our home away from home a little different, unique, and magical.

Every campfire became an opportunity to cook together. We'd sit under the stars, sharing stories about our lives that we'd never had time to do before. These were some of the most romantic and intimate moments we'd ever spend together.

The Duke

ONE OF THE people I had the pleasure of getting to know during my marriage to John Derek was The Duke (John Wayne). He and his lovely wife Pilar would invite us to their home in Newport Beach, then take us aboard Duke's amazing boat, the *Wild Goose*, which, if I recall correctly, was a converted mine sweeper or some other unusual and massive vessel.

Often while we were sailing, John and Duke played chess. Duke would drink mezcal (with the worm) and John his usual whole milk. But no matter how much the big man drank, to my John's chagrin, Duke always checkmated him.

The Duke's Favorite Recipes

Pilar Wayne is a great cook who actually published her own terrific cookbooks. But back when we were fortunate enough to dine with the Waynes, Pilar shared some of Duke's favorite recipes with us that have become mine, too. Here are two of them.

DUKE'S CRAB DIP

MAKES 8 TO 10 SERVINGS

2 (8-ounce) packages cream cheese, at room temperature

5 tablespoons whole milk

2 tablespoons dried onions

1 tablespoon Tabasco

½ teaspoon kosher salt

1 pound lump crabmeat, picked over, any shells discarded

Preheat oven to 350°F.

Put the cream cheese in the bowl of your electric mixer. Beat the cream cheese on low, slowly adding the milk. Keeping the mixer on low, add the dried onions, Tabasco, and salt. Remove the bowl from the mixer and use a rubber spatula or wooden spoon to fold in the crabmeat by hand.

Spoon the mixture into a 1½-quart casserole dish and bake for 30 to 45 minutes, until it's lightly browned on top. Serve warm, with tortilla chips (I make them myself).

If there is ever any leftover (rare . . .), put it in an omelet.

DUKE'S CRAB DIP OMELET

One of the great things about making Duke's Crab Dip is that the next day you can make a terrific omelet with the leftovers. Here's a simple recipe that I discovered for making an omelet. To my surprise, I have never seen it in any cookbook. The broiler is the trick!

MAKES 1 OMELET

Small Omelet: 2 eggs, beaten with a pinch of salt

Regular Omelet: 3 eggs, beaten with a pinch of salt

1 teaspoon unsalted butter

2 to 4 tablespoons Duke's Crab Dip, at room temperature (page 53)

Set an oven rack close to the broiler and preheat the broiler.

In an 8-inch nonstick, broiler-safe omelet pan, melt the butter over medium heat. While the butter is still bubbling, add the beaten eggs.

Cook until the eggs just start to set on the bottom, and then place the pan under the broiler. Broil just a few seconds, until the top is barely set—don't look away! It's preferable to undercook the omelet just a little, as it will continue to cook in the hot pan.

Remove from the broiler and spoon Duke's dip over the eggs in a thin layer. Put the pan back into the broiler just to warm the dip. Then take it out, fold your omelet over, slip onto a plate, and serve at once.

JOHN WAYNE'S FAVORITE GREEN CHILE AND CHEESE CASSEROLE

Pilar says this dish was such a favorite of Duke's that he would take the recipe with him when he filmed on location, folded up in his pocket, so he could have it made for him.

1 pound Monterey Jack cheese, shredded

2 (7-ounce) cans Ortega whole green chiles, drained, patted dry, and cut into ½-inch pieces

1 pound cheddar cheese, shredded

4 eggs, separated

1 tablespoon all-purpose flour

1 (5-ounce) can evaporated milk

½ teaspoon Tabasco

2 medium tomatoes, peeled, seeded, and diced (see page 56)

Preheat oven to 325°F.

In a 2-quart casserole dish, put a layer of Jack cheese, some chopped chiles, and a layer of cheddar cheese. Repeat until all the cheeses and the green chiles are in the dish.

In a medium bowl, beat the egg yolks until thick and lemon colored. Sift the flour over the egg yolks, add the evaporated milk and the Tabasco sauce, and mix to combine.

In a separate bowl, beat the egg whites with an electric mixer until just beginning to form stiff peaks. Gently fold the whites into the egg yolk mixture with a spatula.

Pour half the egg mixture over the top of the casserole. Then, with a metal skewer or a chopstick, poke holes through the casserole so the egg mixture can seep down to the bottom layers. Pour the rest of the egg mixture over the casserole.

Bake uncovered for 30 minutes.

While the casserole bakes, peel the tomatoes by putting them one by one into a pot of boiling water for about 15 seconds. (If they're not very ripe, you may need 30 to 60 seconds.) Lift the tomatoes out with a slotted spoon and put into cold water to stop the cooking. Pull the skin off with the tip of a knife. Cut the tomatoes in half and squeeze to remove the seeds. Chop the tomato into 1-inch chunks and then pat dry with a paper towel.

Remove the casserole from the oven and dot the top with the chunks of tomatoes, pushing them into the top layer. Bake an additional 30 minutes.

After removing from the oven, allow the dish to rest for 15 to 20 minutes before eating so that the cheese is softly set.

Guess Who's Coming to Dinner?

As I MENTIONED earlier, many of John's friends believed that Ursula Andress would one day leave Jean-Paul Belmondo and come back to get my John, because he was the love of her life. The rest of his friends also believed they'd get back together, but they felt it was because she was the love of his life. Not exactly words to warm my heart, especially toward her. So, when John suddenly told me "Urs" was in town and on her way over, I was far from thrilled.

Despite my feisty reputation as Krystle, wrestling Alexis to the ground, I'm really not an aggressive person by nature. However, that day, as I waited for my so-called rival to arrive, I knew she'd have to fight me to get him.

But it's really hard to want to deck someone when you open the door to find her already in tears. "Damn," I thought, "I think I like her. And she's so beautiful, I really pray she's not here to get him back."

Fortunately, she had come to try to save their friendship. Of course I didn't know that until later when Jean-Paul arrived to join us for dinner and I could finally put the "Ursula-will-mess-up-my-life-myth" to rest. And on top of that, I got a new friend.

Damn, she's beautiful!

MY FAMED ARTICHOKE DIP

I've been making my artichoke dip for years. Practically everyone who has ever tasted it has asked me for the recipe. It's perfect for large parties or for smaller, intimate gatherings. Or when your husband's ex-wife comes to dinner! The secret here is to use the artichoke bottoms, not the hearts. Artichoke hearts may be easier to find, but they don't produce the same results. The recipe easily doubles or triples for large gatherings. You can also replace the artichokes with 7 ounces of lump crabmeat for a delicious variation.

MAKES 6 SERVINGS

1 (8-ounce) package cream cheese, at room temperature

½ cup mayonnaise

1 teaspoon Tabasco (or more, to taste)

1½ tablespoons thinly sliced scallions (white part only)

½ cup grated Parmesan cheese (I prefer Parmigiano-Reggiano)

1 (13¾-ounce) can artichoke bottoms (not hearts), drained and finely diced

Preheat oven to 350°F.

With an electric mixer, beat the cream cheese with the mayonnaise. One by one, blend in the Tabasco sauce, scallions, and Parmesan.

Using a rubber spatula or wooden spoon, fold in the artichokes (don't use the mixer for this).

Spoon the mixture into a 3-cup baking dish and bake for 30 minutes, or until golden brown. Serve warm with crackers.

Far from Evil but Scary as Hell

BECAUSE OF HIS love of beauty and photography, John became a brilliant cinematographer, something he learned from Russell Harlan, one of the best cinematographers in the business. Russ was nominated for an Oscar for *To Kill a Mockingbird* and two John Wayne classics, *Red River* and *Hatari!* (one of the reasons my John and John Wayne became friends). Russ was like a second father to John and John named his son Russell in his honor.

News of John's ability with a camera somehow found its way to Evel Knievel, the motorcycle daredevil. Evel was getting ready to do his most challenging jump ever at Caesars Palace in Las Vegas and wanted John to shoot it, so he invited us to come.

John agreed. He also agreed to shoot with two cameras, which meant I would be operating one of them. John had taught me over the years how to shoot a still camera, but now I was about to get a crash course in motion picture photography.

The night before the shoot, we arrived in Vegas to have dinner with Evel. He could not have been nicer, more gracious, or more forthcoming; to the point, Evel admitted that he did not believe he could actually make the jump.

John and I were stunned. John asked, "Then why the hell are you going to do it?"

Evel said that he had given his word; people had flown in from all over the world to see him, so he felt he had a responsibility to do it.

We did everything we could to try and talk him out of it, but he'd made up his mind. John said he didn't want anything to do with it. He wouldn't do business with a man who knew he probably wouldn't make it. But since it was impossible to replace John at this point, he agreed to shoot it, give him the film, and have nothing more to do with his insanity.

John and I went back to our room and I told him there was no way I could sleep knowing what might happen. John said that neither of us would be getting any sleep because we had to rethink our plan. John had expected to be on the camera with the long lens, because it was the most challenging. But now we realized Evel might not complete the jump, and I might not be able to pan with him as he sailed through the air or if—God forbid—he didn't make it. John was determined to give Evel what he wanted, so he had to give me a crash course in how to operate the camera and pull focus with the long lens. Neither of us slept at all that night.

The next day, we set up our cameras at Caesars Palace. One look and we understood why Evel didn't think he could make it: two jump ramps were set on either side of the palace fountains, 141 feet apart. It was absolutely insane, but at this point all we could do was take our positions and pray.

John set up my camera on a tripod at the far end of the jump, the idea being that if Evel made it all the way, I'd be set up to have him in the shot as he was landing on the ramp. The challenge would be keeping him in focus as he was riding straight for me.

John took the side view so he would have to pan along, always keeping Evel in the frame.

At last, it was time for the big event. John signaled me to be ready. From where I was I couldn't see or hear what was happening; even the roar of the bike was drowned out by the roar of the crowd.

Suddenly, there was Evel, dropping toward the ramp. I remember thinking, *Thank God he's made it.* But then, to my horror, he came crashing down, the bike going out from under him! Evel was hurling down the ramp toward me, flipping and twisting like a rag doll. I had no idea what I shot or didn't, all I could think of was that this beautiful man was being broken into pieces.

When he finally came to a stop, we started rushing toward him, but security and medical were already surrounding him. We couldn't reach him. All we could do was watch as the ambulance came and took him away. It was one of the saddest things I've ever seen, but thank God, somehow, Evel did survive.

Later at the hospital, we were greatly relieved when we were able to speak to him and confirm that he was really going to be okay. We still didn't know whether we'd actually captured the jump on film, but John said whatever we got, he was going to give to Evel. He kept his word. In spite of the fact that we needed the money, we signed over all the film rights.

I loved John for doing what he believed was right. And I was thrilled that what I somehow managed to capture on film was what Evel needed from that ill-fated jump: footage that he would one day use in a movie about his extraordinary life.

The Trials of a Bunky

DESPITE THE WARNINGS from John about Bunky and her madcap antics, during my hiatus from *The Big Valley*, I called her and invited her to have lunch. We decided to go to Brown's on Hollywood Boulevard (something that later became a tradition that Bunky and I continued through our *Dynasty* days). We both loved their egg-salad sandwich and their hot fudge sundae.

I picked up Bunky at her house and off we went. It was perfect; there was hardly any traffic on the freeway. Bunky noticed there was a police car behind us. I told her not to worry, I was within the speed limit. Next thing we heard was a voice through a bullhorn telling us to pull over.

"Well, that can't be meant for us," I said. But then the police officer pulled up alongside of us and repeated, "Pull over." And so I did.

Out of the squad car came the youngest policeman we'd ever seen. Bunky whispered to me that this rookie must have just gotten out of the academy yesterday.

When he reached my window, I asked, "What did I do wrong?"

"You were going too slow," he replied.

Stunned, I looked over to Bunky, who leaned across me and got right into the policeman's face. "You're full of shit!" she said, and now *he* was stunned. For a long moment, he and Bunky just stared at one another, neither backing down. Then he asked for my license. He took it and walked back and got into his car. I could see him in my rearview mirror. He was just sitting and glaring at us for what seemed like an eternity.

"What's taking him so long?" I asked nervously.

Ignoring the question, Bunky glanced back and said, "Don't let him think he's gotten to us. Laugh, Linda, laugh!" Then she threw her head back, arms in the air, and laughed hysterically.

Reluctantly I followed her lead, while thinking, "Oh my God, what am I going to tell John? I'm certain I'm coming home with a ticket!"

The young officer returned to my window and, to my surprise, asked, "Can your friend drive this car?" Before I could even respond, he added, "Because I am taking you to jail on a warrant for an outstanding parking ticket."

Bunky couldn't get her mouth open before he said, "And I've called for backup!"

When I was under contract to MGM, they wouldn't allow us to park on the lot, hence the many parking tickets. Parking on the street meant we had to move the car every few hours. I thought I'd paid them all, but apparently one had slipped through the cracks.

When the backup arrived, the new officer put my hands behind my back and cuffed me. He then put me into the back of the squad car and got in beside me—dangerous parking-ticket criminal that I was—to make sure I couldn't make a getaway.

As we headed for the Van Nuys jail, I kept looking out of the back window to be sure Bunky was still following us. When we reached the police station, the rookie suddenly made a sharp turn into the restricted underground parking, ditching Bunky.

They marched me through a series of barred doors, which clanked shut behind us, leading me deeper and deeper into the bowels of the jail. Thankfully, off in the distance I could hear Bunky's faint voice reassuring me, "Don't worry Linda, I'm here!"

They took a mug shot and fingerprinted me. I was horrified. I never broke the law. I wouldn't even jaywalk. I was allowed to make one phone call, just like in the movies. I called John, who was editing his latest film. When he answered, I blurted out, "I'm in jail. I need you to come down and bail me out."

"Very funny. Very funny. You and Bunky are always joking around," he said, and hung up.

Luckily it turned out that I had just enough cash on me to bail myself out of this nightmare.

Stranger than fiction, later that afternoon I got a phone call from the brother of one of my best friends from junior high, who just happened to be a police officer in Van Nuys. Richard told me he'd had lunch with his police buddies and one of them said, "You'll never guess who I just arrested: Linda Evans of *The Big Valley*."

"You must be kidding," Richard said. "She's one of the nicest people I've ever known."

The young rookie responded, "It wasn't because of her—it was her crazy friend."

The good news was that Richard talked him into letting me off the hook. But the rookie had one condition: my crazy friend couldn't be in court. Period. So with great relief, I called Bunky to tell her.

"Oh no, you're not going to court without me. It could be a trick! I'm the witness. I have to be there to protect you!" she said emphatically.

As the court date approached, Bunky's insistence grew stronger and stronger and I caved.

The fateful day arrived. As I turned into her driveway to pick her up, I saw someone come out her front door. Who is that slithering along the wall? It was Bunky, looking like Agent 99 from *Get Smart*. She had covered her long silver hair with a short black wig and was wearing a trench coat and huge sunglasses. She got into the car and said, "Fooled you, didn't I?" It really was a great disguise.

Two blocks before the courthouse, Bunky got out of the car so no one would see we were together.

When I got to the courtroom, I was early and had to wait for them to open the doors. Suddenly, I spotted Bunky pressed behind a potted palm in the hallway and I started to laugh. As people began arriving, they looked at me as if I were nuts. Who laughs before going into court? The harder I laughed, the more Bunky played up her super-spy antics.

Finally the courtroom door opened and I went to the left side and she slinked off to the right.

My friend Richard came in and sat by me. Then the unimaginable happened: the young rookie came in with his backup and they sat directly in front of Bunky. I watched in horror as she leaned up closer and closer, eavesdropping on the rookie's conversation.

"Oh my God, my God, just let me get through this day," was all I could think.

Thanks to Richard, the rookie told the judge that he'd since learned his equipment might have been off. The judge dismissed the charges. Fortunately, Bunky never said a word, so I was free to go.

While we drove home, relieved and laughing, Bunky told me she'd heard the rookie say, "Linda Evans is too thin."

I could live with that. My first caper with Bunky and I survived—but so did my mug shot I suspect.

This may be a good time to explain Bunky, though she isn't quite that easy to explain. She's a force of nature, undoubtedly, but there's so much more to her than her wild side.

Bunky is the most loyal friend you will ever have, and there's a reason she's been my best friend all these years. She has an amazingly positive attitude that can lift you out of anything. She is definitely spontaneous and funny, but she's also fiercely protective of those she loves. If you're lucky enough to be her friend, she's yours forever, no matter what.

Back in the Saddle Again—Almost

HAVING WATCHED ME bouncing around on the sweet old horse they gave me on *The Big Valley*, John decided to share one of his passions with me. He'd practically grown up riding and some of his favorite memories were of playing polo at Will Rogers Polo Field in the Pacific Palisades.

We looked at several horses together before John found the one he was sure would get me as hooked on riding as he was. We arranged to have him shipped to a nearby stable in Griffith Park for boarding. The first time I went to ride him, John got stuck in a meeting, so I went with Bunky.

The day the horse got away.

I came prepared, bearing gifts to win him over: apples, carrots, sugar, a currycomb, and a brand-new saddle. He wanted none of it. Hard as I tried, I couldn't get him to stand still long enough to get the saddle on him. I tried to get Bunky to help, but she just laughed, "No way."

Frustrated, I finally gave up and went home to tell John, who couldn't believe I let the horse win. He made me turn right around and go back with him, to show me "how it's done."

He did. John got the saddle on, then mounted up and went bucking off a few feet before sailing through the air and down onto his butt. I tried to hide my laughter, but it was so perfect to see this great equestrian sitting on his backside in the dirt, the dust still settling around him. For once I got to say, "I told you so."

We later learned that the horse, which was still a stallion, had been drugged when we bought him. The good news is we were able to sell the horse to my stuntwoman from *The Big Valley*, who was able to break him and really loved his spirit.

Semi-sweet Memories

JOHN WAS ALWAYS incredibly romantic throughout our time together. He'd make boots and soft leather clothes for me by hand (much to Barbara Stanwyck's and Nolan Miller's horror). He'd even write me a love letter every night before we went to bed. When I was with John, he made me feel like I was the most important person in the world. So for nine years, I really believed I had a solid, lasting marriage.

We did everything together, including films—partly because I loved being with him, but mostly because John insisted that I stop working for anyone else. Which is why I pretty much disappeared from the public eye. After *The Big Valley,* the only time I worked without John was when his projects weren't bringing in enough to cover our overhead.

John had written many movies, including one I starred in, which we filmed in Switzerland. We decided for the next film it would be better for our relationship if I didn't have to act in it (since John wasn't exactly the easiest director on the set), so he wrote a script called *And Once Upon a Time* to be filmed in Greece. The thought of shooting around the Greek Islands seemed so romantic I could hardly wait to go.

When I first met Mary Cathleen Collins, she was fifteen and already a "ten," even though her name wasn't yet Bo Derek. She came to our house to audition, and I knew the minute she walked through the door she'd get the part.

Ironically, what few people realize is that John and Bo really couldn't stand each other when we started working on the film. They argued about everything from his wanting to dye her hair brown to his thinking she needed to lose weight.

*Cathy Collins, before she was Bo Derek,
with our boy Haji.*

Since Bo had no acting experience yet, John asked me to work with her on the script. So Bo and I spent a great deal of time together, and the two of us did get on very well.

Before leaving for Greece, I told my agent to find me some work, since this was a very low-budget film and the money that John was making was not enough to cover all our bills.

My agent called me in Mykonos to let me know I was offered a guest-starring role in George Peppard's series *Banacek*. The tension between John and Bo had escalated, so I was worried about leaving them alone. I was afraid all they'd do is fight. Two weeks later, when I returned, John had fallen in love with his fifteen-year-old leading lady.

Some part of me couldn't believe that their relationship would last. It made no sense; he was thirty years older than Bo—surely he'd come back.

The Best Revenge

I'VE ALWAYS BEEN an idealist about love. To me, love was what made life worth living. Love and loyalty went hand in hand. So when John left me for Bo I was devastated. I couldn't stop loving him, so how could I go on?

Some people eat when they're miserable. I'm the opposite. I got thinner and thinner, in spite of the fact Sean kept bringing me milk shakes to try and fatten me up. But nothing worked because I'd gotten to the point where I just didn't care anymore. I remember thinking: if God were merciful I'd just get sick and die. Then I wouldn't have to live in such pain. I couldn't imagine life without John.

A few months after we'd split up, the phone rang around five in the morning. I was sound asleep and didn't recognize the voice asking me, "Are you dating yet?" It took me a moment to realize it was John calling from Europe.

I could barely wrap my mind around the question. "Dating?" He didn't ask me how I was doing. He didn't tell me he missed me. He wasn't sorry for what had happened between us. He was only trying to put his mind at ease. Of course if I had met someone else, he would no longer have to feel guilty over everything. That morning, I realized he was not coming back, and I had to start living my life again.

It was a turning point for me. A wake-up call in every sense of the word. I sat up in bed thinking: This is the man I was going to die for? That day, I took my life back. I called my agent and told him I wanted to go back to work.

The minute I took my thoughts off John and back onto me, my whole life turned around. I started eating and stopped looking like the living dead. Almost immediately I had job offers: the first was *Nakia*, a movie of the week with Robert Forster, and then a feature film with Richard Burton.

One of the things I learned, that I would love to share, is that there is life after your man is gone—even though it may not feel like it at the time. For me, an entire new world opened up. Which is why I've found that the best revenge is to get happy.

For me, love doesn't have to end because a relationship does. John and I remained friends until the end of his life.

To this day people still have a hard time believing that Bo and I are also friends. It's true. I believe in my heart that Bo never set out to get John; he fell in love with her. Also, the fact is, Bo did me an enormous favor by totally changing the direction of my life. If I had stayed with John, I would never have had the opportunity to do *Dynasty* and receive all the wondrous gifts that it gave me.

Blessings often come in the disguise of loss. After all, years later I did have my Greek Island romance—with a very romantic Greek called Yanni.

FRESH START BLUEBERRY MUFFINS

Most people don't realize how simple it can be to make blueberry muffins—they're so easy, you could practically make them any morning you want. It's less complicated than some omelets I've started off the day with. Fresh blueberries are key here. They'll hold together in the baking process better than frozen. I use an extra-large muffin pan here, also called a Texas-size muffin pan.

MAKES 6 EXTRA-LARGE MUFFINS (OR 12 REGULAR-SIZED MUFFINS)

1 cup fresh blueberries
1½ cups all-purpose flour, sifted
½ cup granulated sugar

½ teaspoon kosher salt

2 teaspoons baking powder

2 teaspoons ground ginger

1 egg

2 tablespoons unsalted butter, melted, plus additional for greasing

½ cup milk

½ teaspoon lemon zest, finely grated

Preheat oven to 400°F. Butter an extra-large muffin pan
(3¼-inch wide x 1¾-inch deep).

Wash and pat dry the blueberries.

In a bowl, combine the flour, sugar, salt, baking powder, and ginger.
After blending those ingredients, gently stir in the dry blueberries.

In another bowl, beat the egg with a wire whisk, then fold in the melted
butter, milk, and lemon zest.

Add the liquid ingredients all at once to the dry ingredients, and stir only
until the dry ingredients are moistened. Pour mixture into muffin cups
until two-thirds full, and bake 15 to 20 minutes, until golden on top.

A Man of a Thousand Names

MICHAEL GREENFIELD, WHO we affectionately call "Greeny" or "Mad Dog" or "The Green Machine," became my agent shortly before John and I broke up. He remains my white knight to this day. Few agents would have tolerated the way I treated my career, pretty much stopping each time I fell in love. But Greeny was always there to pick up the pieces and somehow find me work. He has become a member of our family.

Michael came into my life after I'd done a guest-starring role on *McCloud* with Dennis Weaver. It was a two-hour movie of the week and the other guest star was Stefanie Powers, whom I'd known from Hollywood High. Last time I'd seen her, I was Linda Evenstad, she was Taffy Paul, and everyone in both our sororities was being suspended from school because of a prank.

In the show, Stefanie and I had such an outrageous catfight that, years later, it became the blueprint for many of the catfights between Krystle and Alexis on *Dynasty*. The day after *McCloud* aired, Michael called saying he wanted to represent me.

I am certainly glad I said yes, because soon after, I was lucky enough to be cast in a film called *The Klansman.*

Breakfast with Burton

ASIDE FROM THE blessing of getting work, I was thrilled to be working with Richard Burton and Lee Marvin. *The Klansman* was one of those movies where the off-camera moments were far more interesting than the film. We were shooting on location in a remote town in Northern California. But when Bunky found out I was working with Richard Burton, we could have been on the moon and it wouldn't have mattered—she was coming to visit me, like it or not!

By the time Bunky arrived, Elizabeth Taylor had left, which I thought would disappoint her, but instead Bunky just felt the field was clear. Keep in mind, she did have four or five husbands—and I don't mean Elizabeth.

On the set the next morning around 8, I needed to run lines with Richard in his motor home. I took Bunky with me. When he opened the door, I thought she would faint. It was like Mark Antony himself had invited us in.

We sat down, and in that charming, eloquent way he had, Richard offered Bunky a drink.

She shot me a look and I knew she was thinking: "Oh my God, I can tell people at home I had a drink with Richard Burton." So, of course, she accepted.

Richard asked: "Vodka?"

Bunky was obviously thinking more like coffee or orange juice at that hour, but she blurted out: "Of course!"

Richard then picked up an 8-ounce glass and filled it to the top with vodka, no ice, no orange juice, just a large glass of vodka. He poured one for himself, toasted, and then proceeded to drink it all down.

It was one of Bunky's rare speechless moments.

LUCIANA PALUZZI'S
PASTA ALLA MATRICIANA

I had many marvelous moments on that film, including working with Lee Marvin for the first time. But the best thing that happened on *The Klansman* was meeting Luciana Paluzzi, a beautiful Italian lady, both inside and out. Like Ursula, Luciana was one of the classic James Bond beauties. She has remained a very dear friend and has given me one of my favorite pasta recipes.

MAKES 6 SERVINGS

2 tablespoons olive oil

½ pound of pancetta (or thick-cut bacon), cubed

One large onion, sliced thin

Red pepper flakes, to taste (as much as your personal desire
   for hot food allows)

6 tablespoons red wine

2 tablespoons red wine vinegar

2 (28-ounce) cans peeled whole or diced tomatoes
   (San Marzano is the best quality)

Salt and pepper, to taste

1 pound penne pasta

Grated pecorino and Parmesan cheese, to taste
   (I prefer Parmigiano-Reggiano)

Heat the oil in a large frying pan and add the pancetta or bacon. Cook until crisp, then pour off about two-thirds of the fat.

Add the onion and the red pepper flakes to the pan, and when the onion is golden, add the red wine and vinegar. Let it sizzle and evaporate for a few seconds, then add the tomatoes, salt, and pepper, breaking the tomatoes up with your spoon. Reduce until most of the liquid has evaporated.

Cook the penne according to the manufacturer's directions. Drain the pasta and pour the sauce over it.

And as Luciana says: "Sprinkle it with the pancetta, cheeses, and love. Serve hot."

Raw Talent

WHEN THE SUSHI craze hit Los Angeles in the 1970s, many of my friends tried to talk me into trying it. The very thought of eating raw anything made me sick. It seemed barbaric. I try to always have an open mind, but in this case my body flat out refused to go along.

Then one day, Christina Belford (who I'd met while working on her TV series *Banacek*) convinced me to go with her to her favorite sushi place. She promised I could eat something cooked if I was too chicken to try something out of the box.

We ended up sitting at the bar at a tiny place, elbow to elbow, and painfully close to the sushi chef and all of his raw delights (a few I'd swear were still moving). I'm not sure how I got through that first time, but some part of the experience must have been okay, because Christina managed to talk me into going back with her.

What I do recall was how delightfully warm and charming the young sushi chef was. He seemed to understand my discomfort and made me very special cooked dishes, while gently encouraging me to try a few well-wrapped, seaweed-disguised raw treats in between. Soon I found myself inviting Christina to join me for sushi.

Looking back, I realize how incredibly lucky I was to be introduced to sushi with undoubtedly one of the greatest chefs of our time, Nobu Matsuhisa. We met long before he owned his first restaurant, the now-famous Matsuhisa, and years before I did *Dynasty*. It was sweet that we became friends before either of us became well known.

Nobu's dishes were so original that it was hard to believe that this genius was in our little neighborhood sushi bar. I introduced my friends

and family to Nobu and we all followed him, like the devoted fans that
we were, anytime he moved to a new location.

I remember how excited I was when Nobu invited me to his home
to meet his beautiful wife and two adorable little daughters. The dinner
was even beyond my expectations. Nobu didn't just study to be a sushi
chef in Japan, he'd also worked in South America. He brilliantly combined the flavors of Peru and Argentina, fusing them with traditional
Japanese cuisine. He was the first chef to do this, and food critics right-
fully launched his career like a rocket.

Courtesy Linda Evans

Chef Nobu Matsuhisa and his beautiful family.

Hundreds of sushi dinners later, Nobu opened his first restaurant
and my career opened up with *Dynasty*. Despite our busy schedules, we
remained friends. The first time I invited Nobu and his family to my
home for dinner, I was shaking in my apron at the thought of cooking
for this amazing chef.

JULIA CHILD'S
"PERFECT" HOLLANDAISE

Nobu loved my hollandaise so much (which I learned from Julia Child and believe is the best there is) that one night at Matsuhisa, he invited me into the kitchen and asked me to show him how to make it. Of course, he did what all truly great chefs do: he played with it and created his own version, which he calls "egg sauce." He was sweet to give me credit for inspiring it in *Nobu: The Cookbook.*

Now Nobu has many great cookbooks and restaurants all around the world. It could not have happened to a nicer, more wonderful guy. Here is Julia Child's classic recipe (reprinted from *Mastering the Art of French Cooking*, with permission).

FOR 1 TO 1½ CUPS HOLLANDAISE—SERVING 4 TO 6 PEOPLE

---

6 to 8 ounces of butter (¾ to 1 cup or 1½ to 2 sticks)

A small saucepan

A 4- to 6-cup, medium weight, enameled or stainless steel saucepan

A wire whip

3 egg yolks

1 Tb cold water

1 Tb lemon juice

Big pinch of salt

1 Tb cold butter

A pan of cold water (to cool off the bottom of the saucepan if necessary)

1 Tb cold butter

The melted butter

Salt and white pepper

Drops of lemon juice

Cut the butter into pieces and melt it in the saucepan over moderate heat. Then set aside.

Beat the egg yolks for about 1 minute in the saucepan, or until they become thick and sticky.

Add the water, lemon juice, and salt, and beat for half a minute more.

Add the tablespoon of cold butter, but do not beat it in. Then place the saucepan over very low heat or barely simmering water and stir the egg yolks with a wire whip until they slowly thicken into a smooth cream. This will take 1 to 2 minutes. If they seem to be thickening too quickly, or even suggest a lumpy quality, immediately plunge the bottom of the pan in cold water, beating the yolks to cool them. Then continue beating over heat. The egg yolks have thickened enough when you can begin to see the bottom of the pan between strokes, and the mixture forms a light cream on the wires of the whip.

Immediately remove from heat and beat in the cold butter, which will cool the egg yolks and stop their cooking.

Then beating the egg yolks with a wire whip, pour on the melted butter by droplets or quarter-teaspoonfuls until the sauce begins to thicken into a very heavy cream. Then pour the butter a little more rapidly. Omit the milky residue at the bottom of the butter pan.

Season the sauce to taste with salt, pepper, and lemon juice.

KEEPING THE SAUCE WARM

Hollandaise is served warm, not hot. If it is kept too warm, it will thin out or curdle. It can be held perfectly for an hour or more near the very faint heat of a gas pilot light on the stove, or in a pan of lukewarm water. As hollandaise made with the maximum amount of butter is difficult to hold, use the minimum suggested in the recipe, then beat softened or tepid butter into the sauce just before serving.

IF THE SAUCE REFUSES TO THICKEN

If you have beaten in your butter too quickly, and the sauce refuses to thicken, it is easily remedied. Rinse out a mixing bowl with hot water. Put in a teaspoon of lemon juice and a tablespoon of the sauce. Beat with a wire whip for a moment until the sauce creams and thickens. Then beat in the rest of the sauce half a tablespoon at a time, beating until each addition has thickened in the sauce before adding the next. This always works.

IF THE SAUCE CURDLES OR SEPARATES—"TURNED SAUCE"

If a finished sauce starts to separate, a tablespoon of cold water beaten into it will bring it back. If not, use the preceding technique.

HOLLANDAISE SAUCE MADE IN THE ELECTRIC BLENDER

This very quick method for making hollandaise cannot fail when you add your butter in a small stream of droplets. If the sauce refuses to thicken, pour it out, then pour it back into the whizzing machine in a thin stream of droplets. As the butter cools, it begins to cream and forms itself into a thick sauce. If you are used to handmade hollandaise, you may find the blender variety lacks something in quality; this is perhaps due to complete homogenization. But as the technique is well within the capabilities of an eight-year-old child, it has much to recommend it.

FOR ABOUT ¾ CUP

3 egg yolks
2 Tb lemon juice
¼ tsp salt
Pinch of pepper

4 ounces or 1 stick of butter

A towel, if you do not have a splatterproof blender jar

Place the egg yolks, lemon juice, and seasonings in the blender jar.

Cut the butter into pieces and heat it to foaming hot in a small saucepan.

Cover the jar and blend the egg yolk mixture at top speed for 2 seconds. Uncover, and still blending at top speed, immediately start pouring on the hot butter in a thin stream of droplets. (You may need to protect yourself with a towel during this operation.) By the time two-thirds of the butter has gone in, the sauce will be a thick cream. Omit the milky residue at the bottom of the butter pan. Taste the sauce, and blend in more seasonings if necessary.

(*) If not used immediately, set the jar in tepid, but not warm, water.

FOR MORE SAUCE

The amount of butter you can use in a blender is only half the amount the egg yolks could absorb if you were making the sauce by hand, when 3 egg yolks can take 8 to 9 ounces of butter rather than the 4 ounces in the preceding recipe. However, if you added more butter to the blender than the 4 ounces specified, the sauce would become so thick that it would clog the machine. To double your amount of sauce, then, pour it out of the blender jar into a saucepan or bowl and beat into it an additional ½ cup of melted butter, added in a stream of droplets.

ASPARAGUS MY WAY

I put Julia's perfect hollandaise on asparagus that I peel before boiling.

¼ to ½ pound asparagus, per person
Salt, to taste
Julia Child's "Perfect" Hollandaise, per person

I think asparagus is better peeled before it is cooked. Using a vegetable peeler or a small, sharp knife, peel up to the green tip. Cut off the dry part of the bottom of each stalk (an inch or more). Then submerge in a large pan of cold water with a dozen or so ice cubes. This refreshes the asparagus and gets it crisp for better cooking.

Fill a large pot with water and set on high heat. When boiling, add salt and asparagus. I differ in taste from most cookbooks in that I cook the asparagus only as follows (because they are peeled they take less time to cook):

Small thin spears: 1 minute

Medium spears: 1½ to 2 minutes

Large spears: 3 minutes

Drain. (As they sit in the colander, they continue to cook.)

Serve with hollandaise sauce or, if you prefer, melted butter.

Take Two

WHEN MY DREAM marriage ended, my life was turned upside down, not only emotionally, but financially. I had no choice but to go back to work. I certainly wasn't ready to date. My friends were persistent, not wanting me to be alone. They kept suggesting men that they thought would be right for me. One bachelor on several of their lists was a play-boy named Stan Herman. Playboy? I don't think so.

One evening at a very elegant dinner in Bel Air, one of my particularly persistent friends surreptitiously managed to seat Stan beside me. It was only after hours of delightful conversation that I found out who he was.

Luckily, I was just preparing to leave for location to do a film, so there was no chance for us to date, even if I decided to ignore my warning voices. But then he became remarkably attentive and thoughtful, sending notes and flowers to me on location. He even proved what a great sense of humor he had, because one day in front of my house (where I'd lived with John) there was a *For Sale* sign from his company, Stan Herman and Associates Realty.

Stan and me in Saint-Tropez.

with John) there was a *For Sale* sign from his company, Stan Herman and Associates Realty.

I never intended to let my-self fall in love with him, but I did when he said he'd waited his whole life for someone like me. I believed him.

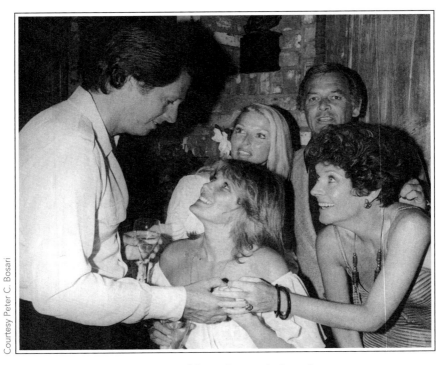

Courtesy Peter C. Bosari

Our wedding day with friends
Dani and David Janssen and Polly Bergen.

We were married on the beach at his home in Malibu on the Fourth of July as the sun was setting. It was so beautiful; I ignored the fact that my friend Christina Belford's mood ring turned black.

Fugitive Found

By THE TIME I met David Janssen, he was already a hero to me. My mother had watched every episode of *The Fugitive*. She was so taken by the show and David that she actually never locked the front door because she thought if the Fugitive wanted to hide somewhere he could stay at our house. Truth.

Sadly, my mother didn't live to meet her Dr. Richard Kimble because I didn't work with David until 1973, well after her death. I did a guest spot on his TV series *Harry O,* which we shot in San Diego, California.

Not long after that, we met again when I started seeing Stan. David was dating Dani Greco and the four of us soon became best friends. Because the four of us had so much fun together, and since David and Dani spent most weekends at our beach house, when the house next door came up for sale they bought it. By then, I'd married Stan, and Dani had married David. We were like family.

David and I even got to work together again on a movie of the week called *Nowhere to Run.* It couldn't have been more perfect. Every morning, when the car came to take us to location, David would come out his front door just as I was coming out mine. Dani would kiss him good-bye, while Stan kissed me, and off we'd go.

I never met anyone who didn't adore David. He had a brilliant quick wit and a mischievous sense of humor. I remember once, during a party in Beverly Hills, we were standing around in a large group, when someone commented how lovely I looked that evening. Without missing a beat, David said, "Of course Linda is beautiful, but have you ever seen her feet?" Naturally everyone turned to stare down at my feet.

One of a kind.

I was wearing high-heeled sandals, which didn't hide the bunion on my left foot. "Yeah, she does have a flaw," David said, shaking his head knowingly. I probably should have kicked him with my bunion, but I was laughing too hard.

Dani and I also got to work together on a project called *Nakia*, starring Robert Forster. Before we did the picture, Dani and I had studied together with Lee Strasberg over the summer when he came to LA to teach. Knowing how bright and charismatic she is, I wasn't surprised that Dani would also be an excellent actress. What the four of us shared was magical. Even after Stan and I broke up, we all remained good friends. Then tragically, we lost David and there was an enormous emptiness in all our lives. To this day, I still miss that guy; he was one of a kind.

Dani and I were often in the kitchen while David and Stan were playing backgammon. Every weekend, more and more friends would come to Malibu to hang out with us, so Dani and I would play around with new recipes to keep everyone happy. Here are two of Dani's recipes that still get rave reviews.

DANI AND DAVID JANSSEN'S CAESAR SALAD

MAKES ¾ CUP

1 egg

1 (2-ounce) can anchovy fillets

1 garlic clove, minced (about ½ to 1 teaspoon)

2 to 3 tablespoons red wine vinegar

1 tablespoon freshly squeezed lemon juice

½ tablespoon Worcestershire sauce

5 tablespoons olive oil

4 small heads romaine lettuce, preferably the hearts
(approximately 12 cups)

½ to 1 cup grated Parmesan cheese (I like Parmigiano-Reggiano),
or more if you love cheese like I do

Coddle the egg by gently boiling it in water for 2 minutes, no longer.

Drain the anchovies (saving 1 tablespoon anchovy oil to mix in the
dressing), then mash with the garlic in a small bowl until a paste is
formed. Add the coddled egg yolk (discarding the white) and blend.
Whisk in the red wine vinegar, lemon juice, and Worcestershire sauce.
Add olive oil and reserved oil from the anchovies in a slow steady
stream, whisking constantly.

Wash, dry, and tear the romaine leaves into bite-sized pieces and put
them in a salad bowl.

Toss the dressing, to taste, with the romaine and ¼ cup of the grated
Parmesan. After distributing the salads on the plates, sprinkle Parmesan
on top and serve immediately.

HAM DANI

This has been one of my favorites. It is a crowd-pleaser that I've served
many times. The leftovers are delicious, because the ham is so flavorful.

1 (13-pound) bone-in ham, skin on

1 (16-ounce) box dark brown sugar, plus 1 packed cup

3½ to 4 teaspoons ground cloves, divided

1 (16-ounce) can crushed pineapple with juice

6 tablespoons instant coffee, dissolved in 2 cups hot water

3 tablespoons prepared yellow mustard, divided

2 teaspoons whole cloves

1 (16-ounce) can unsweetened pineapple rings, for garnish
   (drain and reserve juice)

2 tablespoons unsalted butter

Preheat oven to 250°F and line a roasting pan with foil. Put one large brown paper bag inside another and set the doubled bag upright in the roasting pan.

Sit the ham, fat side up, down into the paper bag, and add the box of brown sugar, 1½ to 2 teaspoons of ground cloves, crushed pineapple with juice, coffee, and 2 tablespoons mustard. Close the bag and tie it shut with kitchen twine. Bake for 4½ hours. (If your ham is a slightly different weight from 13 pounds, bake it 20 minutes per pound.)

Remove from the oven and let cool 10 to 15 minutes. Increase the oven to 400°F.

Carefully cut the paper from the ham, slowly, being very cautious of escaping steam. Pick up the ham with oven mitts and place on a cutting board. Peel off the skin and trim the fat, leaving half an inch on the surface. Score the fat in a crisscross pattern, then place the whole cloves in the corners, pushing the cloves through the fat and into the meat. (If they're not pushed in deep enough, they'll pop out when you glaze the ham.)

To make the glaze, put the remaining sugar, ground cloves, and mustard and ⅛ to ¼ cup of reserved pineapple juice (from the pineapple rings) into a saucepan over medium-low heat and stir just until the sugar dissolves. Immediately remove from heat (do not overcook or it will get hard). Brush most of the glaze all over the ham. Set the remaining glaze aside for basting and finishing.

Add another layer of foil to the roasting pan and place the ham back in the pan. Bake at 400°F for 30 minutes, until golden brown, basting the top every 10 minutes. (Reserve a few tablespoons of glaze to coat the pineapple slices.)

While the ham is baking, pat dry the pineapple slices. Put 2 tablespoons of butter in a frying pan over medium heat and add the pineapple rings. Lightly brown the pineapple rings on both sides, then remove. Put some of the reserved glaze in the pan, adding a little more pineapple juice to thin it. Place the pineapple slices in the sauce, turning to coat them; cook for 3 to 4 minutes on low heat.

After the ham is done, allow it to sit for 10 to 15 minutes before carving. When you have placed the sliced ham on a platter, place the pineapple rings around it and serve.

A Whirlwind Romance—and Lifestyle

LIFE WITH STAN was night and day from what I was used to. John kept his circle close but small; Stan's spanned the world.

While we were married, Stan became partners in Pips, a successful restaurant and disco/backgammon club in Beverly Hills. One of his partners was Hugh Hefner, who I'd known for years. While I was married to John, we'd often go to the Playboy Mansion for dinner and movies.

One Halloween, Ursula, Stan, and I were invited to the mansion for a costume party. Because of my recent breakup with John, there was a lot of press at the time about John's wives, so Urs and I decided to have some fun with it. We dressed up like boxers, one of us with a shiner. The real joke was what great friends we were.

Battling it out at the Playboy Mansion.

The parties we had in Malibu were special to me because of the wonderful new people I was meeting. Almost every weekend, our house was filled to the brim with laughter and great conversations. It was so different from my life with John, where I'd spent most of my time alone with him. Now every night would usher in a new set of guests—friends like Suzanne Pleshette; Altovise and Sammy Davis Jr.; Ginny and Henry Mancini; Polly Bergen; Alana and George Hamilton; Ann and Richard Harris; Leslie and Tony Curtis; Liza Minnelli and Jack Haley Jr.; Bridget and David Hedison; Sandra and Tony Bennett. People would start dropping by at midday and often stay until the wee hours of the morning.

With Stan I experienced a lot of freedom. It didn't bother him if I worked; he even encouraged me to work. It was such an incredible time of change. I adored this new life with Stan. It was so much more in-line with who I was.

Courtesy Linda Evans

Real-life dancing with the stars,
with Tony and Leslie Curtis in Malibu.

We both loved being with people, and now I could always invite my friends over and cook their favorite meals for them. We'd have big buffets during the summer, but during the winter months the group would be smaller so we could eat around the fireplace in the living room.

Fireside friends Corinna and Freddie Fields, Dani, and David.

CHICKEN, SHRIMP, AND MUSHROOMS

Another crowd-pleaser, this dish I invented can go a long way when you're feeding a house full of invited and unexpected guests. (Just multiply the ingredients so that each diner has one breast, three shrimp, and two mushrooms.) Easy and delicious, this was always a favorite during my Stan days.

MAKES 4 SERVINGS

1 pound (4 sticks) unsalted butter, at room temperature

3 tablespoons melted butter for the mushrooms

6 tablespoons soy sauce

6 tablespoons freshly squeezed lemon juice

1 teaspoon minced garlic

8 large white mushrooms

4 chicken breasts, skinless and boneless

12 colossal raw shrimp (12 count to a pound), peeled,
    cleaned, and deveined

Make the seasoned butter: Place the room-temperature butter in the bowl of an electric mixer or food processor, and gradually beat in the soy sauce, lemon juice, and garlic, adding a few tablespoons at a time.

Preheat the broiler.

Spread a thin layer of the butter mixture on the bottom of three broiler-safe glass dishes (an 8 x 8-inch, a 12 x 9-inch, and an 11 x 7-inch).

Discard the mushroom stems and clean the caps by wiping them with a damp paper towel. Dip each mushroom in the melted butter to coat, and place them, hollow side up, in the prepared 8 x 8-inch dish. With a spoon, fill the mushroom caps with the seasoned butter.

Place the chicken breasts in the prepared 12 x 9-inch dish and spread them generously with the seasoned butter.

Place the cleaned shrimp in the prepared 11 x 7-inch dish and generously spread the seasoned butter over each.

Broil the mushrooms.

Cook them on one side only: 3 to 4 minutes for small ones, 4 to 6 minutes for large.

Broil the chicken. Cook small breasts on the first side for 4 minutes, 5 minutes for large. Spread a little more seasoned butter on the chicken after turning. Cook the second side for 3 minutes for small breasts, 4 minutes for large.

Broil the shrimp. Cook the first side for 2 minutes for small shrimp, 3 minutes for large shrimp. Spread a little more seasoned butter on the shrimp after turning. Cook the second side 1 to 2 minutes for small shrimp, 2 to 3 minutes for large.

Timing is the most important thing with this recipe; cook the items in this order, and don't overcook. The butter not only keeps everything moist, it also continues to cook the food once it's removed from the oven.

After they all come out of the broiler, some of the butter mixture will have separated. Spoon ¼ cup of butter from the chicken pan and put it into a small saucepan over the lowest heat possible on the stovetop. Heat briefly, remove promptly from the heat, and then whisk in about ¾ cup of the uncooked seasoned butter, which will then form a creamy sauce. Do not overheat, or it will separate again. Put the sauce in a gravy boat.

Put the chicken, shrimp, and mushrooms on a serving platter and pass the butter sauce separately.

Moon River, Wider Than a Smile

NEAR THE END of summer when it became cooler in Malibu, friends would gather for lunch around the roaring fire in our living room. Often by sundown, it would become so packed with people, I'd find myself slipping upstairs for a tiny moment alone before shifting gears for dinner.

The upstairs master bedroom was a wonderful place to sit and relax, looking out over the ocean. I remember one evening walking into my bedroom and feeling like I wasn't alone. As I rounded the corner, I saw Henry Mancini sitting on the bed, taking in the beauty of the moon as it cast its spell on the water. Like minds.

Dani Janssen, Anne Harris,
Alana Stewart, and me Dressed To Kill.

I quietly sat beside him. The next moment the door opened and Alana walked in. I chuckled as she sat on the other side of Henry. All three of us wanted to be alone. We sat silently enjoying the music that played throughout the house.

Then the most perfect thing happened: "Moon River" started playing. I flashed on Audrey Hepburn in *Breakfast at Tiffany's*. Alana started singing and then Henry and I joined in. It was such a magical moment, sitting there with the composer of this beautiful classic. They didn't even mind that I was off-key.

Enter Nena

WHEN I FIRST met Nena she was this shy little lady from Belize who was hired to be our housekeeper. But I realized very quickly that she had great instincts for cooking. She did in fact become a great cook, as well as a part of my family for the next twenty-eight years.

I remember one of the first times Nena ever served drinks for us in Malibu. Stan asked her to go see if anyone in the Jacuzzi wanted a cocktail.

Off Nena went with her little silver tray, only to stop cold when she found Tony Curtis, Sammy Davis Jr., and Ted Kennedy in the bubbling water. The guys saw that she was flustered and sweetly told her they'd each like a Screwdriver.

Nena hurried to the kitchen to ask what to do. The cook, who was afraid Nena would one day replace her, promptly told her to go to the closet and look in the toolbox.

While Nena was wrestling with the enormous toolbox, Stan walked up wondering what the hell she was doing. Totally rattled, Nena blurted out the whole tale. After a good laugh, Stan taught her how to make a Screwdriver and sent her back to the Jacuzzi with her silver tray.

When she arrived, the three gentlemen stood up to get their drinks, which Nena nearly threw into the air, because all three were naked and saluting her. Somehow she managed to serve them, then beat a hasty retreat straight into the kitchen, where she informed the cook that if anyone else in the Jacuzzi wanted a drink, the cook could serve them herself.

LESLIE AND TONY CURTIS'S LEMON SOUFFLÉ WITH RASPBERRY SAUCE

Tony and Leslie were regulars at our house in Malibu and we shared many great dinners with them at their beautiful home in Bel Air. Being a lemon lover, I asked them for this recipe.

MAKES 6 SERVINGS

LEMON SOUFFLÉ CURTIS

4 lemons

5 egg yolks

1½ cups granulated sugar

2 packages unflavored gelatin

2 cups heavy whipping cream

6 egg whites

⅛ teaspoon salt

⅛ teaspoon cream of tartar

Grate the lemon zest (you should have about ½ cup) and juice the lemons (1 cup).

On the top of a double boiler over gently simmering water, beat together the egg yolks, the sugar, the lemon zest, and the lemon juice. Cook, stirring constantly, until the mixture has thickened enough to coat a spoon. (This will take a little while.) Remove from the heat. Take the pan out of the simmering water and put the lemon mixture in a large bowl.

In a small bowl soak the gelatin in ½ cup of room temperature water. Stir to mix. Then add the gelatin to the warm lemon mixture and blend well. Set aside to cool.

When the lemon mixture is at room temperature, whip the cream until soft peaks form and mix it into the lemon mixture.

Beat the egg whites with the salt and cream of tartar until stiff peaks form. Fold half of the whites into the lemon mixture gently, to lighten the base, and then gently fold in the other half. Pour mixture into an 8-cup soufflé dish.

Refrigerate at least 4 hours.

Serve with raspberry sauce.

RASPBERRY SAUCE

Here's a really easy, delicious sauce you can make without ever turning on the stove.

MAKES 2 CUPS

2 cups raspberries
2 tablespoons granulated sugar
1 teaspoon freshly squeezed lemon juice

Mash ¾ of the raspberries through a large fine-mesh strainer, discarding seeds. (You can also puree them in a food mill, and then strain to remove the seeds.) Mix in the sugar and lemon juice.

Mash the remaining berries with a fork and stir into the pureed berries.

Refrigerate for at least an hour to chill through, and serve cold.

FROZEN RASPBERRY SAUCE

MAKES 1½ CUPS
---

2 (10-ounce) packages frozen unsweetened raspberries

2 tablespoons granulated sugar

1 teaspoon freshly squeezed lemon juice

Place the frozen raspberries in a strainer suspended over a bowl, to thaw. Mash the thawed raspberries through the strainer to remove the seeds. Discard the juice and seeds. In a small bowl, mix the puree with sugar and the lemon juice.

Not So Tuffy

EVEN THOUGH STAN and I had been married a while, I was still driving the '67 Jaguar that John had bought for me in Switzerland during my very first trip to Europe.

Stan didn't like my having any reminders of my past, so he asked me what my favorite car was—besides the old Jag I was driving. I told Stan that there was one car that I thought was absolutely beautiful, an older classic Mercedes that I had dreamed about owning. Stan said he didn't want to get me a used car; he wanted a new one with all the warranties. So for my birthday he gave me a brand-new, beautiful, little black Mercedes convertible coup. I was touched by his generosity, but a part of me still dreamed about the old classic.

Life works in mysterious ways, because if I had gotten my dream car, I would have really been depressed a couple of months later. I had been visiting Stan at his office in Beverly Hills. Parking was always at a premium, but I'd found a spot in the lot running parallel to the old railroad tracks. As I was pulling out I saw a lady waiting with her blinker on. Suddenly another car whipped around to try and steal her spot. I was so appalled that I decided to ease back into my space until the unethical man went away. But in my unnerved state, I accidentally hit the gas pedal and my new, super-powerful little Mercedes literally flew over the parking meter and onto the railroad tracks, where I sat in stunned horror while the man pulled into my space laughing his head off.

Later, as we watched (with the amused crowd that had gathered to see the little Mercedes somehow trapped sideways across the Beverly Hills train tracks), I was very relieved that Stan wasn't angry. Instead, he just laughed at the absurd situation and how totally flustered and embarrassed I was.

Believe me, at that moment, I certainly wasn't thinking life never gives you a problem without a gift. But as always, it was true. A few weeks later, Stan was looking at a Rolls-Royce that he was thinking of buying for himself from Sonny and Cher, when Sonny asked him if he happened to want to pick up an old Mercedes, too.

Stan called me and said, "Come to this address, I want to show you something." When I arrived, Sonny asked for the car to be brought around, and the second I saw it, I started to cry.

© Ron Galella/Getty Images Entertainment

Stepping into my dream come true.

It was exactly what I'd dreamed about down to every detail, from the cream color, to the elegant burl wood and camel leather. It was as if the car had been waiting for me since the day it rolled off the assembly line.

Sonny and Cher had so many cars they hardly ever drove it. So this beautiful old Mercedes was like new.

Once again, life was showing me that if I can hold onto my dream, it will eventually come to me—even if sometimes it drives up in the most outrageously unexpected ways.

After my railroad track incident, Stan decided my nickname should be Tuffy, or at least it would be good if people thought I was tough, so he ordered a vanity plate with "Tuffy 9" on it, the number nine being a favorite of mine, not that there were nine of us "tuffing" it out on the streets of Beverly Hills.

I loved my Tuffy dearly. Every time I'd see Sonny around town, he'd always ask if I'd sell him back the Mercedes. It was a standing joke between us, but we both knew there was no way I was giving up my dream car.

An Avalanche of Mixed Memories

GREENY OVERHEARD THE producers at Lorimar arguing over what to do about a well-known actress they were trying to negotiate a deal with for a new feature, due to start filming soon. She was apparently being very difficult. So Michael offered them a simple solution: take Linda, who you love to work with, and forget the temperamental actress.

So off to Germany I went to begin filming *Avalanche Express*. It was a wonderful, international cast, featuring talents like Lee Marvin,

Men in black and me—on location with
Lee Marvin, Robert Shaw, and Horst Buchholz.

Robert Shaw, Mike Connors, Maximilian Schell, Horst Buchholz, and Joe Namath.

I arrived in Munich a couple of days ahead of most of the cast, so I found myself eating alone in the hotel dining room. Then one evening, Mike Connors and his wife Mary Lou came in, and from that moment on the making of *Avalanche Express* became one of my fondest memories.

We immediately hit it off. Mike is one of the funniest, most charming, and outrageous characters I have ever met. He could be Bunky's twin. Mary Lou and Mike have an enviably romantic relationship. I could be walking along with them through the lobby of the hotel, when suddenly, Mike would take Mary Lou in his arms, dance a couple of Astaire-esque steps, then dip her to the ground, leaving the crowd cheering.

In the evenings, we'd often sit around the piano bar and Mike would hop on the piano and start singing "Strangers in the Night." Mike's fun-loving spirit was so contagious that one night Joe Namath joined him. I would have, too, but I didn't want to clear out the bar with my singing.

If our little group wasn't entertaining enough for us and all the people filing into the piano bar to see Mike, Ursula showed up, too—she had come in from Rome to visit me. Ursula already knew and had worked with most of the cast, so it was like old home week for most of them.

It was also wonderful having the opportunity to work with Robert Shaw, who, aside from being a truly brilliant actor, was a lovable, warm, charismatic gentleman. He had a keen wit and outrageous sense of humor. I'm sure Robert would have joined Mike at the piano bar if he hadn't brought his wife and three children on location. But that was another thing I adored about Robert: that he wanted his family with him, even when he was working.

I had invited Stan to join me on location, but he didn't come until the end of filming. I had heard a lot of rumors about all the parties he was having after I left. I had begun to sense something—something I just didn't want to let myself believe. I was in deep denial. I kept telling myself: There's no way I could have done this again. There's no way this was going to happen to me again.

When I returned from Germany, I couldn't hide from my suspicions anymore, and my friends confirmed them for me. Stan was still a playboy. And now I had to ask myself: Did I want a husband who said he loved me and wanted to stay married to me, but who intended to be with other women? Of course I didn't.

After my marriage to Stan ended, I was left with a horrible sense of sadness. It was more about me and my choices than anything else. Here I was, thirty-seven, and my dream of a lasting marriage with children was further away than ever. What was going on with me? Why was I not able to have those things I most wanted?

This was another turning point. For the first time in my life, I took a hard look at myself to figure out who and what I was all about. I kept myself from being distracted. I stayed away from books, newspapers, movies, and TV. I didn't go out or see friends. I needed to turn my focus completely on myself to try to find some answers. What I discovered was the part I was playing in my failed marriages.

Through self-contemplation, I realized that what was standing between me and my dream was an old thought pattern. It started when I was in my late teens; I fell in love for the first time. During our relationship, he got someone else pregnant and married her. After that, I linked love and betrayal and it became a pattern I unconsciously lived. In seeing it, I could let it go and replace it with a new one that better served my dream.

Once I understood my pattern, I never repeated it again . . . only faithful men in my life since then . . . thank God.

Life without Marriage,
but Not without Love

WHEN I BECAME social again, many of my friends did their best to make sure I wasn't alone, especially during the holidays. The first Christmas after my divorce, Roger and Luisa Moore invited me and the Hedisons to their wonderful home in Gstaad, Switzerland, to spend the holidays with their family. It was like stepping into a Christmas card, being in the Alps, with all the beautiful chalets covered in snow. That Christmas I felt very fortunate and grateful to be with a loving family and friends instead of being at home wondering why I couldn't seem to get the marriage thing right.

Bridget, David, and me at
Roger and Louisa Moore's house in Gstaad, Switzerland.

110

One of the sweetest memories I have of that trip is when Roger made a traditional English Christmas pudding, which he mixed a coin into before baking. Whoever finds the coin gets blessings for the year. I found it. I always wondered if he might have rigged it my way, but however it happened, I did get many blessings that year.

BÛCHE DE NOËL

This is the dessert my family likes me to make every Christmas. The die-hard chocolate lovers like it with the icing drizzled over it. The rest like it without, so I usually make two. It freezes well . . . if there are any leftovers. My thanks to Diana Welanetz Wentworth for teaching me this recipe.

MAKES 6 TO 8 SERVINGS

1 6-ounce package semisweet chocolate chips (1 cup)
1½ teaspoons instant coffee
3 tablespoons water
5 eggs, separated
1¼ cups sugar, divided
1½ teaspoons vanilla

FOR THE FILLING:
1 8-ounce carton whipping cream
1½ teaspoons vanilla
2 tablespoons powdered sugar

FOR THE ICING:
½ cup powdered sugar
1½ tablespoons Hershey's unsweetened cocoa
1 tablespoon hot water

¼ teaspoon instant coffee

¼ teaspoon vanilla

1 tablespoon melted butter

Pinch of salt

Preheat oven to 350°F. Grease an 9 x 13-inch jellyroll pan.
Line it with wax paper, and then grease the wax paper (I use Crisco).

Place chocolate chips, 1½ teaspoons instant coffee, and hot water in
a double boiler over gently simmering water until melted, stirring
occasionally to combine. Remove from heat and cool to room temperature.

While the chocolate is cooling, beat the egg yolks, ¾ cup of the
sugar, and 1½ teaspoons vanilla in a large mixing bowl until thick and
pale yellow.

Slowly fold the cooled chocolate mixture into the egg yolks.

In a separate bowl, use an electric mixer to beat the egg whites until
they form soft peaks. Then gradually add the remaining ½ cup sugar,
a small amount at a time, until the meringue forms stiff peaks.

Use a rubber spatula to fold one-third of the meringue into the
chocolate mixture to lighten the base. Then slowly, with the rubber
spatula, fold the rest of the meringue, a little at a time, into the
chocolate mixture—like you would when making a chocolate soufflé.

Gently spread the mixture into the jellyroll pan and use the spatula to
smooth it to the edges of the pan.

Place in the oven and bake 17 minutes. Don't peek. Remove the cake
from the oven to cool. (The cake will fall and crack like a failed soufflé.
Don't be horrified—it's supposed to!)

While the cake cools, make the filling by whipping together the cream,
vanilla, and powdered sugar until soft peaks form.

Gently slide a spatula between the jellyroll pan and the waxed paper to separate it from the pan. Spread a clean kitchen towel over the top of the cake and flip the whole pan upside down, holding the towel tight to catch the cake as you flip. Carefully peel the wax paper off the surface of the cake.

Spread the whipped cream filling over the surface of the cake and then roll it up like a jellyroll using the towel to help you lift and roll. Now you should have the classic Christmas *bûche*, or "log." With two spatulas, one on either end of the log (pointing toward the center) very carefully lift onto a serving dish. The log will look cracked and broken.

To make the icing sift the powdered sugar and cocoa through a fine mesh strainer, using the back of a spoon, into a small bowl. In another small bowl combine the hot water, instant coffee, vanilla, and *hot* melted butter, stirring well. Add the warm ingredients to the powdered sugar/cocoa combination, whisking until blended. *Immediately* drizzle the icing along the very top of the log. (Do not make this too far in advance, because the icing will get stiff because of the butter.)

Refrigerate until you are ready to serve. You can make and assemble it up to 5 hours in advance. Any leftovers freeze perfectly.

The Part That Didn't Get Away

THE FIRST TIME in my life that I actually wanted a career was after my second divorce. I had invested in some real estate with Stan while we were married. I didn't want alimony from him, but I did want to buy a small house in Beverly Hills that he owned and I loved. So I put my investment money toward it. There was still a sizable mortgage, and if I couldn't make the payments, I'd lose the house. That's exactly the way I wanted things, because I needed that fire under me so I would fight like hell to get my career back on track. I was counting on the adversity to make me strong, not take me down. I knew it wasn't going to be easy, but I was determined to make it on my own.

One of the first opportunities that came up was huge: an interview with Steve McQueen for a film he was starring in and producing, a true story titled *Tom Horn*. I was very excited, until Steve opened the door and, looking extremely uncomfortable, immediately told me that he was sorry I came, because I was wrong for the part. Not the response I was hoping for. But then he did soften the blow by saying it was because he thought I was too attractive, and he was looking for a more believable frontier woman. But then he said: "Oh well, you're here, come on in." The old adage, just get your foot in the door, is true. I got the part!

This film was very important to Steve, and he really took it over, down to the last detail. He selected every piece of fabric—dowdy and drab—for my wardrobe. He even met me at the dentist when they made my gold tooth (to give me the frontier woman look).

On location, a few days before filming, the unthinkable happened: I got laryngitis because I was so terrified—I needed this job and they had already replaced a few of the actors. Steve was very kind. "Linda," he told me, "I want you to know I totally understand," was all he said. He didn't want me to talk to anyone or speak for any reason for a week so I could get back my voice.

Westerns have always been my favorite: I love being outdoors, the animals, the down-to-earth nature of the wranglers, stuntmen, and cowboys. But *Tom Horn* holds a very special place in my heart, because acting with Steve was one of the greatest experiences in my career. He was so brilliant when he was performing that I'd get lost in his performance and nearly forget my next line.

Even better than I imagined.

It was a wonderful time for me, filled with firsts, including the day Steve called me aside while on location in Tucson, Arizona, plopped a plate of mashed potatoes in front of me, and said I was getting too thin. Believe me, I never thought I'd hear that one in Hollywood.

Then again, when I think about it, this might just be a Western thing, because years later, when I did *The Gambler* with Kenny Rogers, he'd have pizza delivered to my room. No wonder I love doing Westerns!

LOSE-YOUR-FIGURE POTATOES WITH CHEESE AND GARLIC

In memory of dear Steve, here's one of my favorite high-calorie and delicious potato recipes. This one is always a huge hit. I like to assemble the cheese and potatoes several hours in advance and cover with plastic wrap, keeping at room temperature before baking. If you do this, be sure to leave the cream mixture covered in the fridge and pour over the potatoes just before baking.

MAKES 4 TO 6 SERVINGS

1½ to 1¾ pounds red potatoes, peeled

Unsalted butter, for greasing

3½ cups grated sharp cheddar cheese (about 12 ounces)

2 tablespoons grated Parmesan cheese (I prefer Parmigiano-Reggiano)

1⅓ cups heavy cream

1 small garlic clove, minced (about ½ teaspoon)

¼ teaspoon kosher salt

⅛ teaspoon white pepper

Put the whole, peeled potatoes in a large pot and add just enough water to cover. Boil until tender, about 20 minutes. Drain and cool. When cool, slice potatoes ¼-inch thick.

Preheat oven to 350°F.

Butter the bottom of a 2-quart (11½ x 8 x 2-inch) baking dish and layer in half the potato slices. Sprinkle with half the cheddar and half the Parmesan. Layer on the remaining potatoes and sprinkle with remaining cheese.

In a bowl, combine the cream, garlic, salt, and pepper.

When ready to bake, pour the cream mixture over the potatoes and bake 40 minutes, until the top is golden brown. Serve warm.

Nearly Disappearing
into a Black Hole

UNFORTUNATELY, *TOM HORN* wasn't the box-office success that I had hoped. Steve had shared with me early on that he was making this picture for himself, not the studio. He'd done the big films they'd wanted; this time he was doing a story he felt passionate about.

So I was back to trying to figure out how I was going to make a living acting. A few months passed without any work, not even a guest spot on TV. Things weren't looking too good. Even Greeny was getting nervous and wondering why I had to wait until I was thirty-seven to finally decide to have a career.

No matter how bad it looked, I kept telling myself it was going to work out, even if everyone else thought I was crazy. And then it happened. Greeny called, all excited: "They are doing a movie at Disney, *The Black Hole*. It's nine months work, right here, no location. You've worked for the studio, the director, and two of the leading men. This could be the big break we've been waiting for."

I was already thanking God for this blessing as I drove to the studio to meet with everyone. It could not have gone better. Well, except that I didn't get the part.

Greeny was crushed. I was shaken, but still holding to my belief that life had something wonderful in store for me. So when, a couple of months later, we learned that the actress they had cast for *The Black Hole* was being replaced and they wanted to see me again, I thought, Yes, I knew it had been a test of my faith, and I hadn't given up.

I went back to meet with everyone, had another great meeting, and then they gave the part to Yvette Mimieux.

This time I was stunned, but I didn't have the luxury of getting depressed, because I knew I would lose my house if I didn't succeed. I still believed that I didn't deserve to fail. The God that I loved didn't punish that way. I realize now that I was doing "the law of attraction" before I knew what it meant. I had absolute faith in my future in spite of "my age."

Even Greeny became a believer when I was rewarded beyond anything I could imagine. Not a nine-month movie, but a nine-year hit series called *Dynasty* that would change my life forever.

By the way, if I'd gotten the part in *The Black Hole*, I would not have been available to shoot the pilot for *Dynasty*.

I'll never forget my first meeting with Aaron Spelling. I was excited and hopeful, but I never dreamed that within a few days, Aaron would tell me I'd be playing Krystle Carrington. What was also surprising was that Aaron asked if I would wear the little diamond cross I had on during filming, because he felt it suited Krystle's character. I gladly wore it for the first year of the show and continued wearing it for many years after, until Yanni's mother, Felitsa, admired it and I put it around her neck.

Aaron had a very dry wit, which I experienced shortly after he and the show's creators, Esther and Richard Shapiro, gave me the part. He said that we wouldn't start filming right away, which was great for me because I was leaving in a week for Aspen to take skiing lessons. I had a condo and an instructor all lined up. Aaron just smiled and said, "Have a great trip. We'll be happy to replace you if you break your leg."

Needless to say, I canceled my ski trip. I didn't reschedule it until last year, when I spent many, many joyous hours on the bunny slopes learning to ski. I'm happy to report no broken bones.

As it turns out, I could have broken both legs and healed them by the time we shot the two pilots and endured a lengthy Screen Actors Guild strike.

Friends for Life

I HAD JUST begun *Dynasty* and Bunky had just divorced her umpteenth husband, so she was free to begin a new career as my personal assistant. However, neither of us were too sure how long the show would run, so Bunky moved into one of my guest rooms for the first season. Ursula came from Europe to visit and took the other bedroom, and from that point on the laughs just kept coming. My home was constantly filled with joy and madness, which drew a stream of friends and family like magnets.

Bunky was in heaven when one of Ursula's regular visitors turned out to be her *second* fantasy man, Sean Connery.

Needless to say that when Sean came over to sunbathe by the pool with Ursula, neither Bunky nor Nena got any work done. Who could blame them?

There's been a lot of media about the unusual friendships between John Derek's four wives, but even John thought it was funny when I invited Ursula to stay at my house during the last month of her pregnancy. It was a little unusual for sure, but there was a good reason. Ursula had made a movie with Harry Hamlin called *Clash of the Titans* and they had fallen in love. Ursula was living with Harry in his house in LA, which had some steep steps. The doctor decided it would be safer for Ursula to live somewhere else, so I invited her to stay with me.

On May 19, 1980, the big day arrived. Bunky and I prayed we didn't end up behaving like everyone in the classic *I Love Lucy* episode: can't find the suitcase, the car won't start, total mayhem. I ended up driving Ursula to the hospital while Bunky located Harry, who was shooting a film at the time. It all came together beautifully. Harry, Bunky, and I waited together for the blessed event. A beautiful boy, Dimitri Alexander Hamlin, was born. How many ex-wives could share something so magical?

When Dimitri came into the world, we made these wonderful fresh fruit desserts. With a new baby in the house, who has time to make anything complicated? The following are two simple, easy-to-make recipes.

STRAWBERRIES AND DECADENT SAUCE

This elegant combination is so much more than the sum of its parts. Everyone loves it.

MAKES 6 SERVINGS

1 cup heavy cream
2 cups buttermilk
¾ cup granulated sugar
½ teaspoon vanilla extract
2 pints strawberries, stemmed and sliced
¼ cup confectioners' sugar

In a mixing bowl, blend the cream, buttermilk, sugar, and vanilla together until incorporated. Pour into an 8 x 8-inch Pyrex dish and chill in the freezer until firm on the edges but not frozen (the center will jiggle), about 1½ hours.

Put the strawberries in a bowl and sprinkle with the confectioners' sugar. Turn with a spoon gently until all the sugar is evenly distributed. Chill in the refrigerator for 15 minutes (no more or it will pull the juice out of the strawberries and make them soupy).

Divide berries among six dessert bowls.

Use a mixer or an emulsion blender to beat the almost frozen cream until smooth. Spoon a ¼ to ½ cup of the sauce over the chilled strawberries, and serve immediately.

WARM BERRIES IN CUSTARD

This dessert is easy to make yet classic. Typically you make this with just strawberries or raspberries but I've added blueberries or peaches. Just be sure that the berries or fruit are cut or sliced small enough that you get a good combination of berry and custard flavor with every spoonful. You can assemble the fruit in the dishes several hours in advance and then add the custard just before serving.

MAKES 6 TO 8 SERVINGS

4 cups berries or fruit, room temperature, cut or sliced

1 cup heavy cream

2 egg yolks

½ cup confectioners' sugar, plus a few tablespoons extra for dusting

1 teaspoon vanilla extract

1½ tablespoons Chambord (or raspberry-flavored) liqueur

Preheat oven to 400°F.

Divide the berries among eight (4-ounce) ovenproof ramekins or six (6-ounce) ramekins.

Whip cream until soft peaks form. Add the egg yolks, ½ cup confectioners' sugar, and vanilla and continue whipping for another minute.

Sprinkle a little liqueur over each ramekin. Pour the custard mixture over the fruit in each dish and place the dishes on a baking sheet in the oven. Bake 3 minutes. Remove the ramekins from the oven.

Preheat the broiler.

Transfer the ramekins to the broiler and broil until light golden brown, watching carefully.

Put a few tablespoons of confectioners' sugar in a sieve and lightly dust each ramekin. Serve immediately.

Love Never Ceases

THE YEAR JOHN Derek turned fifty-two we decided to celebrate him by giving him a birthday party. Ursula, Bo, and I started planning the event. Sean got some of the photos that John had taken of each of us and we had custom T-shirts made.

We brainstormed a menu and Ursula reminded us that chili was one of John's favorites.

The loves of John's life.

The night before his birthday, Ursula, Bunky, and I met in the kitchen. It was great fun. We all chopped and participated in the creation. Hours later, and a few glasses of wine, Ursula suggested we add bourbon to the chili. Bourbon? Bunky and I had never heard of that trick. It tasted delicious.

What were we thinking?

The next day we were busy wrapping our gifts, writing our cards, and decorating the house. Two hours before the party I went into the kitchen and discovered that the chili had never been put in the refrigerator. It had sat out all night and had spoiled. It had to be thrown out. Oh great, now what do we do?

If at first you don't succeed, get a can opener! Thank God for canned chili. It saved the party. No one was the wiser. Most important, John felt loved and he was.

The Derek wives gathered to celebrate John's life once again after he passed away. Bo invited us to the private memorial for him at their home in Santa Ynez. The day was filled with laughter and tears as many shared their stories about him. He would have loved seeing us all together again. Love never ceases. He will always be a part of my life.

The wives and Sean together at John's memorial.

An Italian Love Affair

I OFTEN MARVEL at how life works. Shortly after I shot the second pilot for *Dynasty*, I was sitting with Ursula having lunch one afternoon when out of the blue she said, "Every woman should have a love affair with an Italian at least once in her life." All of us who know and love Ursula always expect her to be outrageous and speak her mind. Even so, this time she caught me off guard. I just laughed because there was no way I would even entertain the idea of picking a lover based on nationality.

A few months later, shortly before *Dynasty* aired, I was stopped at a red light on Sunset Boulevard. I heard a horn honking and turned to my right to see an incredibly handsome man in a jeep motioning me to roll down my window. "You've got a loud noise coming from your carburetor and if you don't get it fixed you could end up with serious problems," he said.

Then he casually told me his name was George and that he owned an Italian restaurant called Santo Pietro's in Beverly Glen. "Come up sometime, we have great food!"

As the light changed I said, "Oh okay, thanks," while I was thinking, *Wow, what a strange way to meet a good-looking Italian. . . .*

Weeks later, Bridget Hedison and I planned to have dinner in one of the restaurants up in Beverly Glen. I'd told her the story about my encounter with the handsome Italian. Bridget suggested we check it out because she'd heard Santo Pietro's had great food. We walked over and discovered a charming little place with candles and romantic music and delicious smells coming from the kitchen. But George was not there.

As we were walking out (with my wondering whether I was relieved or disappointed), we decided to walk down to the new sushi restaurant a

Georgio and me at Hazen.

few doors away, which she'd heard was great, too. And there was George. He and I looked at each other and said in unison: "Mercedes. Jeep."

Since he was standing behind the sushi bar, I was confused. "What are you doing here?" I asked. "I thought you owned the Italian restaurant."

"I do. And I own this place, too," George replied. Then he invited Bridget and me to sit down.

As I watched this charming, charismatic man pouring us sake, I wondered if this could be my "once-in-a-lifetime Italian." As fate would have it, he was. And by the way, there was nothing wrong with my car. Which could just mean he was a lousy mechanic. The good news was that he turned out to be a wonderful chef who taught me lots of great recipes. George and I cooked together in my kitchen in Beverly Hills with Nena. She adored George and was in heaven anytime he cooked with us. He'd suddenly take her in his arms and dance around the kitchen with her. I loved that side of George; he'd often ask sweet old ladies at his restaurants to dance between courses. They would light up because they could tell he genuinely enjoyed it, too.

What Goes Up Must Come Down

ASIDE FROM COOKING, George's greatest passion was flying, a hobby he discovered when we were first together. When George put his mind to something, he did it all the way, which is probably why he was an A student and why his flight instructors respected him so much.

Once he got his pilot's license, I was the first to go up with him (much to the horror of flying-phobic Bunky). After that, George's romantic side would come out and he'd call to say, "Let me fly you to the moon!" And he did many times.

My "fly me to the moon" man in the cockpit.

One afternoon, a few months after he'd gotten his license, George needed to fly to Northern California for a business meeting and wanted me to come along. As we were preparing to take off, it was clear that weather conditions weren't ideal. The rain had stopped for the moment, but the winds were still strong. I felt apprehensive for an instant, but then it passed because I had such confidence in George's ability and he didn't seem concerned. Well, that is until we were nearing the airport and he told me that he'd heard there was a very steep mountain at one end and a very short runway with a forest on one side. Aside from how difficult the mountain made the approach, if there was wind, it had to be coming from a certain direction for a "successful landing."

In other words, this was one very tricky airport to maneuver, even when the weather was good. It looked like we were in luck. The tower gave George the okay to land, which meant the windsock was in our favor. But George wasn't happy with his first approach and decided to abort rather than take any chances. So we went back up.

We circled several more times waiting for the tower to tell us the wind was right again. I was starting to get a little nervous. But finally we got the okay to come in.

Just as we were touching down, the wind suddenly shifted, but it was too late to abort. We were already barreling down the runway with the wind pushing us forward like a rocket. Up ahead I could see a chain-link fence with traffic speeding along on the other side of it.

Already knowing the answer, but hoping anyway, I looked over at George and, with surprising calm, asked, "That's the end of the runway, isn't it?"

"Yes," he answered with equal calm.

"We're going to crash aren't we?"

"Looks like it." George replied.

An instant later, his survival instinct kicked in and he turned the plane so sharply to the right that it pulled us off the runway and onto the rain-soaked grass. We avoided crashing into the fence and speeding cars, but the second the tires hit the grass, the plane flipped over and came to a jarring stop.

Hanging upside down from the ceiling in my safety harness, I felt incredibly relieved. I looked over at George hanging next to me and almost laughed because we looked like two bats. But then George said we had to get out of the plane immediately because it might explode.

Without another word, we both unbuckled our belts as fast as we could and, at the exact same time, landed on our heads. The crash didn't hurt us, but we nearly killed ourselves trying to get out. Rubbing our heads and moaning, we crawled out of the plane together.

Already we could hear lots of emergency vehicles coming. I suddenly flashed on all the warning I got from the studio about taking unnecessary risks and realized that the press could have a field day with this. The last thing either of us needed was for this to end up on the front page of the tabloids. George was going to have enough to deal with.

Right before the fire engines reached us, I took off to hide in the woods that flanked the airport. There was so much chaos surrounding the crash; miracle of miracles, no one ever found out I was there.

Hours later, George and I were able to reunite and take a commercial flight home. He told me that they had suspended his license until a formal investigation into the crash was completed.

It took quite a while, but eventually George was not only exonerated but also the truth about this particular airport was finally brought to light. There had been several other crashes, most not as fortunate as us; those planes actually hit the chain-link fence and people were killed. As with us, the tower would okay a landing, only to have the wind shift so quickly there was nothing a pilot could do. So, as usual, there was a purpose for good in this, too; because of our crash, the airport was closed and no one else would ever be hurt there again.

I Was Never One of Charlie's Angels, but He Was Sure Mine

JOHN FORSYTHE WASN'T actually the first Blake Carrington on *Dynasty*. In the original pilot, George Peppard played my husband. However, by the end of filming, there was so much discord between George, Aaron, and the network that they mutually agreed to release George from his contract.

After George left, Aaron looked to John Forsythe. They had worked together when John did the voice of Charlie on *Charlie's Angels*. John had also just received critical acclaim for his riveting performance in . . . *And Justice For All*.

My first speaking part, with John Forsythe (when we were both brunette).

The stars had all lined up to give me the best star in the world to work with.

When we returned to Northern California to reshoot the pilot, it was wonderful to see John again (who, by the way, was responsible for giving me my first speaking part at age fifteen on a show he produced and starred in called *Bachelor Father*). He was more handsome than ever. He walked up to me on the set and said, "My, little Linda Evenstad, how you have grown. How is your mother, Arleen?" I loved him for

131

remembering my mother. What a charmer. He made every day on *Dynasty* more memorable than the last; this continued for nine years. There was only one John Forsythe. I was so lucky to have him in my life.

Astaire couldn't do it better.

A Man for All Reasons

DURING THE COUNTLESS hours of daily *Dynasty* drama, John never failed to make me laugh. Not only was he easy to love, but he was also a fine actor and a total professional. He was my cheerleader . . . well, that is when he wasn't making me laugh in the middle of my close-up.

John had a brilliant sense of humor. When we would shoot elaborate and elegant dinner scenes, which meant hours of sitting around a table, we'd all start to fade or get restless, so John would invariably come up with something to snap us out of it and get us laughing. Whether it was telling one of his classic old jokes, or suddenly appearing off camera wearing my chandelier diamond earrings. As you can imagine, Bunky and John Forsythe were instant lifelong friends.

No wonder we were always fighting over this gorgeous guy.

133

One of my favorite memories of John's wit happened during an interview we were giving together between filming. It was for a major national magazine and the reporter was very serious and professional. John responded in kind, keeping the gentleman spellbound with his usual eloquence, while guiding us across the set to where a classic, headless Greek statue rested at the end of a hallway.

When we reached the stone goddess, John paused, as if in deep contemplative reflection, and put his hand right on her breast. The reporter just stared, stunned. As the silence continued, the poor man started to squirm, obviously at a complete loss for words. John never faltered, but I nearly exploded from the laughter I was holding back.

The interviewer never mentioned it in his article. I still smile to this day when I think about it.

The Jewel in John's Life

IT SHOULD COME as no surprise that John was married to an exceptionally wonderful and talented woman. The real surprise to most was that Julie was famous before John. They met while she was starring on Broadway in Cole Porter's *Around the World*. She was a beautiful woman with an amazing singing voice. But like so many women of her generation, she gave up her career for her man.

I first met Julie when John and I started working on *Dynasty*. I knew immediately that we were going to become good friends. The three of us ended up traveling all over the world and always shared wonderful times together. Often we'd talk Julie into singing for us. Her voice was so beautiful and pure; she didn't even need any accompaniment. Everyone

John Forsythe and his two wives.

135

loved hearing her, but what was most touching for me was to see how John always looked at her, with such great love and pride.

Sometimes Bunky would travel with us and at the end of the evening we'd end up in one of our suites in our pajamas with Champagne and dessert. John would go off to bed saying he needed his beauty sleep, leaving his "angels" behind. Julie, Bunky, and I would stay up for hours sharing stories and laughing.

John and Julie were married in the early 1940s and shared a great, solid marriage until her unexpected death in 1994. I will miss her always.

JULIE FORSYTHE'S SESAME CHICKEN

Shortly after we lost Julie, I went to visit John in Santa Ynez at their ranch and their family cook of forty years, Toyoko, made one of Julie's recipes for us. This is my version of it.

MAKES 4 SERVINGS

6 tablespoons (¾ stick) unsalted butter, divided

4 chicken breasts, boneless and skinless, cut into 1-inch strips lengthwise

¼ cup grated Parmesan

¼ cup sesame seeds

1 cup breadcrumbs (preferably panko)

Kosher salt and pepper

2 eggs

2 tablespoons milk

½ cup all-purpose flour

Canola oil for frying

Melt 4 tablespoons of butter on low heat and pour into a large bowl. Add the chicken strips and turn to coat them fully. Set aside.

In a shallow dish, combine the cheese, sesame seeds, breadcrumbs, ½ teaspoon salt, and ¼ teaspoon pepper. In another shallow dish, beat the two eggs with the milk. On a plate, combine the flour with ¼ teaspoon of salt and ¼ teaspoon of pepper.

Heat ¼ inch of oil along with the remaining butter in a large skillet over medium heat.

Dip a chicken strip in the flour, turning to coat both sides well. Then dip the strip in the egg wash, followed by the breadcrumbs, turning the strip to coat well each time.

Lay the breaded strip in the hot oil, and repeat with three to four more strips (you can dip two at a time to fill your skillet quickly).

Cook 4 to 5 minutes altogether, turning once, until golden brown. (If the strips are browning too fast, lower the heat.)

Remove the cooked chicken to a paper towel–lined plate and cook the remaining chicken. Serve at once.

Golden Opportunities

WHILE I WAS doing *Dynasty*, I ended up doing several other shows because I realized how lucky I was to be offered the opportunity to work with legends like Bob Hope. I actually did three specials with Bob. I cannot say enough wonderful things about this remarkable man. I loved working with him and I was grateful he gave me the opportunity to do comedy.

The most outrageous skit I remember was in one of the earlier shows, and it wasn't as much about the script as the stunt Bunky decided to pull. The skit was a spoof on the highly successful *Shogun*, the miniseries with my old friend Richard Chamberlain. Loni Anderson, Barbara Eden, and I were cast as Shogun Bob's adoring geishas.

When Bunky went to see our wigs, which were on three wig stands, she decided that the one with my name on it wasn't the best looking. So later, when no one was around, Bunky snuck in and switched the nametags. This is a long overdue apology, but sorry Loni—Bunky didn't tell me until after we were done shooting.

In all honesty, it was as much my fault, I suppose. Because whenever Bunky gets that devious twinkle in her eye and can't wait to tell me what she's plotting, I always hold up my hands and insist: "Whatever it is, I don't want to know."

The last Bob Hope special I did was in Paris, which was an added bonus, but I would have gone to the ends of the earth for another chance to laugh and work with Bob.

Bob and his geishas: Loni Anderson, Barbara Eden, and me.

Nothing Like My Sweet Little Kitties; or, Circus of the Fools

IN THE FIRST year or so of *Dynasty*, we still weren't sure how long we'd be on the air, so any time an opportunity came along to make some extra money, I jumped on it. I actually ended up working most weekends for the first couple of seasons.

Greeny decided that *Circus of the Stars* would be good exposure for me, but Bunky was adamant that I not do anything ridiculous: "Linda isn't doing any stinking poodle act. It has to be something really exciting or forget it."

The producers called to let us know that there was a leopard act in the Midwest that sounded perfect. The next weekend, Bunky and I flew out to the middle of nowhere to meet Sheba, a two-hundred-pound leopard, and her trainer. Bunky and I agreed that the leopard was very impressive. So I worked with Sheba that evening, taking her through her routine, which went very smoothly.

Later, when we were flying home, even though we were exhausted, Bunky was really thrilled that I wasn't doing something lame or tame. She said, "Now this is an act you can sink your teeth into."

Sheba landed the job, so *Circus of the Stars* brought her to Los Angeles to work with me. She arrived during a brutal heat wave, which turned the San Fernando Valley into a 113-degree oven. As I was getting ready to leave for my first rehearsal with Sheba, Bunky suddenly decided she had much too much work to do in the nice chilly air-conditioned office. I was on my own.

I'd imagined there would be at least a tent between the scorching sun and us, but instead they set up a few staggered pedestals out in the open.

Courtesy Circus of the Stars

Me and Sheba when we were still friends.

I had a hoop for Sheba to jump through and a little whip to convince her who was boss. But after the first command, it was clear Sheba wasn't buying it. Her trainer told me I had to be more assertive with the leopard; this wasn't one of my sweet little kitties at home. She also made it clear that when you are dealing with a wild animal, you must take control right away. Easier said than done. Being someone who won't even step on a spider, I wasn't comfortable hitting Sheba with the whip, even if it only was on her paw. But everyone insisted that it was the only way.

Sheba was up on a pedestal that put her just above my head. Next thing I knew, I had a leopard leaning down and roaring right in my face. She was inches from me and she and I both knew who had won. But the trainer still insisted that all I needed to do was gain Sheba's respect.

I'm not one to give up easily, but it was clear neither of us was having much fun; plus, I really didn't want to hurt her. Thankfully, she didn't really want to hurt me either—otherwise, a moment later, when she leaped off the pedestal and drove me onto my back with her teeth in my chest, she would have killed me. For a moment everyone thought she might have, but then Sheba simply stepped away from me, while all hell broke loose.

I guess I was in shock because it took me a while to realize what had happened. I was more upset by the fact that Sheba had torn my favorite shirt than that one of her teeth had punctured my chest. Even though I really felt like I was okay, they rushed me to the hospital, where they bandaged my chest and gave me a tetanus shot.

Later, with my shirt in tatters and my now black-and-blue chest heavily bandaged, I returned to my air-conditioned home to find Bunky sipping wine and chatting on the phone. I just stood in the doorway staring at her until she finally looked up. After her initial horrified reaction, she said, "Very funny. Nice try, but I'm not falling for it."

I didn't say anything. I just continued staring at her. When she finally realized it wasn't a joke, Bunky went crazy and wanted to hunt down Sheba and her trainer (they fortunately had disappeared without a trace right after the incident). When Greeny found out, he wanted to hunt Bunky down for not being there to throw herself in front of the cat instead of nearly getting his client killed.

The good news was, not too long after my ordeal with Bunky, Greeny, and the other wildcat—I realized that I might not need to be doing so many sideshows.

Forty Isn't Fatal, It's Fabulous

TURNING FORTY IS supposed to be stressful, but I loved it. Much to Greeny's horror, I have always admitted my real age. As I turned forty, I realized I wouldn't go back to being younger. I had earned wisdom, which more than compensated for the downside of aging.

I also ended up having one of the most romantic birthdays of my life, since George arranged to take me on the legendary Orient Express from Paris to Venice.

The train was classically elegant, a true work of art. I felt like we had stepped back in time: everyone was beautifully dressed for dinner, the staff and waiters all saw to our every need. The food was unforgettable; all the dishes were prepared on the train by French chefs.

Yes, turning forty turned out to be wonderful.

Around that time I did a commercial for Clairol and in it I announced to the world, "Forty isn't fatal."

I loved that Joan Collins and I were older than most leading women on TV and that our characters were portrayed as glamorous and vital. I thought it was a wonderful message for women everywhere.

Turning forty also helped me to look at my life from a different perspective. It became very clear to me that my biological clock was ticking, ticking, ticking, and I was still holding to the dream of having my own family. While George and I adored each other and loved cooking and traveling together, we both knew we wouldn't be together forever. It was time for us to get on with our lives and just be friends.

Romance on the Orient Express.

INA GARTEN'S
FILET OF BEEF BOURGUIGNON

The Barefoot Contessa is one of my all-time favorite cookbooks, and Ina's version of Filet of Beef Bourguignon is one I have been making for years. It's easily something that could have been served on the Orient Express during that wonderful birthday adventure! It cooks quickly and the filet is so incredibly tender. A special thanks to Ina Garten and her publisher, Clarkson Potter, for allowing me to share this recipe with you. Copyright Ina Garten. All rights reserved.

MAKES 6 TO 8 SERVINGS

1 3-pound filet of beef, trimmed

Kosher salt

Freshly ground black pepper

3 to 4 tablespoons good olive oil

¼ pound bacon, diced

2 garlic cloves, minced

1½ cups good dry red wine, such as Burgundy or Chianti

2 cups beef stock

1 tablespoon tomato paste

1 sprig fresh thyme

½ pound pearl onions, peeled

8 to 10 carrots, cut diagonally into 1-inch-thick slices

3 tablespoons unsalted butter at room temperature

2 tablespoons all-purpose flour

½ pound mushrooms, sliced ¼-inch thick (domestic or wild)

With a sharp knife, cut the filet crosswise into 1-inch-thick slices. Salt and pepper the filets on both sides. In a large, heavy-bottomed pan on medium-high heat, sauté the slices of beef in batches with 2 to 3 tablespoons oil until browned on the outside and very rare inside, about 2 to 3 minutes on each side. Remove the filets from the pan and set aside on a platter.

In the same pan, sauté the bacon on medium-low heat for 5 minutes, until browned and crisp. Remove the bacon and set it aside. Drain all the fat, except 2 tablespoons, from the pan. Add the garlic and cook for 30 seconds.

Deglaze the pan with the red wine and cook on high heat for 1 minute, scraping the bottom of the pan. Add the beef stock, tomato paste, thyme, 1 teaspoon salt, and ½ teaspoon pepper. Bring to a boil and cook uncovered on medium-high heat for 10 minutes. Strain the sauce and return it to the pan. Add the onions and carrots and simmer uncovered for 20 to 30 minutes, until the sauce is reduced and the vegetables are cooked.

With a fork mash 2 tablespoons butter and the flour into a paste and whisk it gently into the sauce. Simmer for 2 minutes to thicken.

Meanwhile, sauté the mushrooms separately in 1 tablespoon butter and 1 tablespoon oil for about 10 minutes, until browned and tender.

Add the filet of beef slices, the mushrooms, and the bacon to the pan with the vegetables and sauce. Cover and reheat gently for 5 to 10 minutes. Do not overcook. Season to taste and serve immediately.

To make ahead: This dish is excellent made in advance and refrigerated in the pan. When you are ready to serve, heat the filets and sauce over low heat for 10 to 15 minutes, until heated through.

TIP:
To peel the pearl onions easily, first blanch them for a minute or two in boiling water.

Quick Draw McEvans

IN *THE GAMBLER* with Kenny Rogers, I portrayed a bounty hunter masquerading as a saloon girl. I had to learn to "quick draw," which required practicing as often as I could. Bunky would work with me for hours at the house between running lines. I'd wear the holster and gun all day, never certain when Bunky would suddenly leap out from behind a door or couch shouting, "Draw!" It was like living with Cato in one of *The Pink Panther* films.

One time during these sessions the doorbell rang and without thinking, I opened the door with the gun in hand. The poor FedEx man stood rooted in fear until I quickly told him I was just practicing for a film.

Before starting *The Gambler*, I was scheduled to do a special two-hour *The Love Boat* in Greece and Turkey. The studio made me a wooden gun so that I could continue to practice and not freak out everyone on the boat.

We had only two days between finishing *The Love Boat* and reporting to *The Gambler* location in Arizona. At long last it was time for me to actually draw on camera. To everyone's surprise I was faster than my character was supposed to be in that scene, so the director needed me to slow down. Yesss! Bunky was very proud.

For me, the most challenging part of *The Gambler* was the singing and dancing. Being a great singer and songwriter, Kenny Rogers assured me that no matter how I sounded, they could fix me in the studio. Wanna bet? Once again I was dubbed. Trouble is, even when an actor is dubbed, they still do actually perform the song in filming before it gets dubbed. So I had to belt out the song in my own poor little off-key

Dressing up in the Wild West.

voice, while I watched Kenny trying to stay in character, struggling not to laugh.

But I'd still have to do my own dancing. Since there was no choreographer on site, Bunky stepped up to the task and soon put together a terrific little routine for me to do. Since we didn't have time to practice it, she had to stand behind the camera dancing away, with me trying to mirror her steps. Not only did Kenny and the crew get a big laugh over our antics, the scene came out great.

Clowning it up on The Gambler.

I absolutely loved working with Kenny and Bruce Boxleitner, and my old friend David Hedison as well. The only hard part was going from shooting *The Love Boat* in the mild Mediterranean climate of the Greek isles to 113 degrees in the Arizona desert. It was incredibly hot and dusty, plus I often had to wear heavy dresses with corsets. I'd get so thirsty that I would race to the craft services table morning, noon, and night. Normally I'd just have water, but I tried their lemonade and found I couldn't stop drinking it. I loved it. After the tenth glass, I told the craft services man that they may have to let my dress out, but I couldn't stop drinking it. He said, "Don't worry, it's diet." He told me it was a new product being test-marketed in the area, called Crystal Light.

Ironically, when I got back to LA, Michael called and said there was a new product called Crystal Light and they'd like to send me some samples to try.

I told Michael they didn't need to send it, I already had it. He said that was impossible because it wasn't out yet. I had loved it so much I'd bought a few cases in Arizona and brought them home with me. I was even making frozen lemonade bars out of it.

Needless to say, I was happy to accept their offer to become their first spokesperson.

George Burns and Other Sex Symbols

GRACIE ALLEN'S
CLASSIC RECIPE FOR ROAST BEEF

1 large roast of beef
1 small roast of beef

Take the two roasts and put them in the oven.
When the little one burns, the big one is done.

SADLY, I NEVER got to work with George Burns's wife Gracie. To this day I love her brilliant funny mind. I did have the great pleasure of doing *George Burns and Other Sex Symbols*.

This was the title of the special I did with the lovable and seemingly ageless George, which aired just as *Dynasty* was taking off in 1982. I was thrilled to be asked to be on the show; until I found out they wanted me to sing "Happy Birthday" to him. Over the years, I've been *seen* singing in films, but trust me: no one has ever actually *heard* me sing.

The first time I was asked to sing was in a Disney film called *Those Calloways*. This is how badly I sing: I didn't even have a solo; I just needed to sing along with the family. One note, and they knew they had to dub me.

Then, I played a bikini-wearing, skydiving singer in *Beach Blanket Bingo*. If that wasn't embarrassing enough, I had to break into song the second I hit the sand. Thankfully, they had the good sense to use someone else's voice. And then there was my experience with *The Gambler*.

So, when I was asked to sing for the legendary George Burns, I begged him to give me something else to do. With his trademark cigar on the side of his mouth, George smiled and said he knew I could do it. Wanna bet?

Bunky had to push me all the way to the studio, since I was absolutely horrified that I was about to make a complete fool of myself in front of the millions who were sure to tune in to see George Burns.

In the end, George saved me by suggesting I just talk-sing, like Marilyn Monroe did to President Kennedy. Of course, I'm no Marilyn, but somehow it got me through. As a matter of fact, it turned out to be a wonderful experience: nothing like overcoming your fears in front of one of your idols, not to mention a few million people.

I Love *The Love Boat*

⁂

EARLY IN MY *Dynasty* days, I agreed to do a few two-hour *The Love Boat* specials during our hiatus. I'd shoot the interiors in the studio and then fly to exotic places all over the world to film on different ships. I loved going to Australia and the Fiji islands, as well as Greece, where we filmed on the islands of Mykonos and Santorini. But my favorite trip was when I went to China. They cast John Forsythe, Ursula Andress, and Lee Majors for that episode as well. We all had shared such sweet memories throughout the years. It was fun for us all to work together.

John's wife, Julie, came with us, and on our days off we went "china" shopping. We'd come back to the hotel with assorted bags filled with our great antique porcelain treasures, which John had to carry and store away on the plane. All the way home he made us laugh with his "typical husband" routine.

My affair with Chinese cuisine really took off when I appeared in *The Love Boat* in Asia. I couldn't get enough of the flavors of Chinese food and combed the stores for all the spices I could take back. We had many unforgettable dinners in Beijing and Shanghai that inspired me to get a wok and learn to cook Chinese cuisine.

One evening a small group of us went to a restaurant close to our hotel. They surprised us with an assortment of appetizers, but we didn't recognize anything. Everyone just stared. Not wanting to be rude by asking what everything was, I adventurously plopped one thing in my mouth only to find it could not be chewed or swallowed. I later found out it was a duck's webbed foot! I still love Chinese food, but, needless to say, I now always ask what I'm eating!

KUNG-BAU CHICKEN
WITH PEANUTS

This is one of my favorite Chinese recipes that I found in *The Classic Chinese Cook Book*. I am very grateful that Mai Leung has been gracious enough to allow me to share it with you. Mai Leung mentions you can cut down on the hot chili pepper; I use just a little and it is delicious.

MAKES 4 TO 8 SERVINGS

PREPARATION OF INGREDIENTS

2 cups oil

⅓ cup raw skinless peanuts

CHICKEN MIXTURE (MIX AND MARINATE IN A BOWL)*

1½ boned, skinless chicken breasts: cut into ⅓-inch cubes (to make 1 cup)

¼ teaspoon MSG (optional)

1 tablespoon cornstarch

¼ teaspoon salt

¼ teaspoon sugar

½ egg white

4 dried chili peppers: tear into small pieces, do not discard seeds

1 tablespoon finely minced fresh ginger root

2 scallions: cut into pea-sized pieces, including green part

SAUCE MIXTURE (MIX IN A BOWL)*

2 tablespoons black soy sauce

1 tablespoon Chinese Shaohsing wine or pale dry sherry

2 teaspoons Chinese red vinegar or cider vinegar

½ teaspoon salt

½ teaspoon sugar

2 teaspoons sesame seed oil

½ teaspoon cornstarch

Heat oil in wok and deep-fry peanuts until golden brown. Drain on paper towels.

Reheat oil in wok and add chicken mixture. Stir to separate pieces. Briskly blanch chicken pieces until they just turn white. Remove with a drainer or slotted spoon to a bowl.

Remove all but 2 tablespoons of oil from the wok. Heat oil. Slightly brown chili peppers. Add ginger and scallions, and stir-fry until they turn golden. Stir in sauce mixture. Cook and stir until sauce is thickened. Put the chicken back into the wok. Mix well. Stir-fry briefly to reheat. Add the peanuts. Mix well and put on a serving platter. Serve hot.

*This sign means that portion of the recipe can be prepared several hours in advance.

PLAIN RICE

MAKES ABOUT 6 CUPS OF RICE

2 cups long-grain rice: wash and rinse in cold water until water is
   not cloudy, drain
3 cups cold water

Use a 3-quart pot with a tight lid. Put in the washed rice and add the water. Cook over medium heat without a cover. When it is boiling, you will see that the water is very foamy, almost obscuring the rice. Do not go away! Stand by and watch it closely. You will see the water evaporating to the point where many small holes (like craters) appear in the rice. The Chinese call them rice eyes.

Put the lid on, turn heat to very low, and cook for 10 minutes. Then turn off heat, but do not remove the pot or uncover it. Let it stay covered for 15 minutes or more. (Do not peek during this 25 minutes! Otherwise the magic steam will escape; you will have half-cooked rice for not having faith!)

Remove the cover. Loosen the rice with a fork or chopsticks. Serve hot.

Angel of Death

DURING THE SECOND season of *Dynasty*, the writers decided that Krystle should have a miscarriage. If that wasn't painful enough, they added a dream sequence, during which Krystle had to give up her baby to the "Angel of Death." I prepared myself for a long difficult day of nonstop crying.

Much to my surprise and delight, the producers thought Bunky would make the perfect Angel of Death, and they hired her for the part. Knowing Bunky always delivered, they often gave her small roles to play on the show.

I knew this would be a piece of cake for Bunky. With her long silver hair and some white makeup, she'd turn this into an Emmy Award–winning performance. I'd seen her scare all the kids at Halloween with her Wicked Witch imitation. This was right up her alley.

After hours of preparation, the stage was finally set for the dream sequence. The lights were dimmed and the mists began to rise. With my *Dynasty* family surrounding me, I stood holding my newborn baby (which was actually a little doll wrapped in a blanket).

The director yelled "Action!" and out of the mists came the Angel of Death, moving toward me. Through a blur of tears, I watched my baby being taken away from me.

Pamela Sue Martin and Al Corley (who played my stepchildren) and John all knew how emotionally exhausting these kinds of scenes could be, so they were being very supportive. Everything was going smoothly. Everyone was into it.

Unfortunately there were technical problems, too much mist for one take or not enough for another. We kept at it for hours, until everyone was exhausted.

But around take fifteen, it all came together. The director asked us to do just one more to see if we could do it even better.

Once he yelled "Action!" Bunky approached me with her arms outstretched as she always had. For all the other takes, I had made sure to keep my eyes on the baby and to not look at Bunky. But for some reason this time I couldn't stop myself from looking up. Big mistake! The Angel of Death was making the most outrageous face imaginable. I was trying desperately not to lose it when suddenly Bunky yanked the doll out of my hands and threw it to John, who caught it like a football. Then he went right along with Bunky's madness and ripped off the doll's leg! Then John tossed it to Pamela Sue, who threw it to Al. The crew got into the melee, too; soon arms and legs were flying everywhere. No doll repair shop could put the doll back together.

The cameras kept rolling and I kept crying, but this time they were tears of laughter after one of the longest, toughest days of filming—but one that we all talked and laughed about for a very long time.

The Joys of Having
Two Dysfunctional Families

DYNASTY OPENED THE world for me in every way. I've thanked God endlessly, but I owe a special thanks to Angie Dickinson for turning down the part of Krystle. Since then, we've become friends, so I was able to thank Angie myself.

Just like a real dysfunctional family, there was always so much drama to be had, and we had so much fun with it—especially during the famous catfights between Krystle and Alexis. The first time I read a script

I may look sweet, but don't mess with me!

that had our characters fighting, I was thrilled to be back to the stunts I so enjoyed doing during *The Big Valley*. Lucky me.

The first stunt was Krystle confronting Alexis in her cottage. It was a knock-down, drag-out fight with feathers flying everywhere. We fought our way through the entire room, knocking over everything in sight, including each other. I won!

Another one of my favorites was the lily pond scene, which we filmed at an estate in Pasadena. Oh, the magic of television. It looked like we were in six feet of water but in reality we were in only two and a half feet, and fighting on our knees! It felt absurd and we struggled all day to make it look authentic. When at the end of the day the director yelled "Cut and print," we stood up looking like a couple of drowned rats. The crew spontaneously broke out in applause and laughter. What fun!

The audience always looked forward to these confrontations and so did I. Joan loved the verbal fights—I hated them. I loved the physical confrontations—she loathed them. We did them all—for nine years!

Take this!

159

The Tuna Meltdown

ANY UNION SHOW always has what we call a craft services table, which is covered with all sorts of drinks, foods, snacks, and candy. What was particularly great about the people doing our craft services on *Dynasty* is that every day they made a large bowl of tuna salad and provided lettuce, tomato, and different breads so we could make our own customized sandwich. John and I would always make a beeline for it, along with half the cast and crew. We all loved it.

One day, word came down that there would be no more tuna because of budget cuts. John and I were both amazed by how upset everyone was by the news; it became the topic of almost everyone's conversation. The show was obviously doing great in the ratings and more and more money was being spent on elaborate sets and wardrobe. So why deny the crew their tuna?

I remembered that Aaron had told me that if I ever needed to talk to him, all I had to do was pick up the phone. I did and was delighted when within a few minutes I was sitting in front of him. I pleaded our case and he kindly sympathized, but firmly stated that the accountants had to make cuts and the tuna was out.

So I told Aaron, fine, if that was the case, then from now on John and I would pay for everyone to have their daily tuna. Aaron was silent for a long moment, just staring, not looking happy. Finally he said, "You know I can't let it get out that the stars of the show have to pay for the crew's food." With a sigh he gave in. We could have our tuna and eat it, too.

DYNASTY CORN PUDDING

Aside from the tuna, one of the *Dynasty* caterers served a corn pudding that many members of the cast and crew—including me!—flipped for. They were kind enough to share it with me. This is how I make it.

MAKES 6 SERVINGS

4 ounces (1 stick) unsalted butter, melted, plus additional for greasing

3 cups fresh corn kernels (from 4 to 5 ears)

2 eggs

1 cup sour cream

9 ounces Monterey Jack or Pepper Jack cheese, cut into ½-inch cubes

½ cup cornmeal

1 (4-ounce) can whole green chiles, seeded, patted dry, and cut
   into ½-inch pieces

1½ teaspoons salt

½ cup grated Parmesan cheese (I prefer Parmigiano-Reggiano)

Preheat oven to 350°F. Generously butter a 2-quart rectangular casserole dish.

In a blender or food processor, puree 1 cup of the corn kernels with the melted butter and eggs.

In a large bowl, combine all the remaining ingredients except the Parmesan. Add the pureed corn and blend well. Pour into the prepared dish, sprinkle with Parmesan cheese, and bake 30 minutes, until puffed and golden. (If the top isn't browned but the pudding looks set, run it under a preheated broiler for a couple minutes until golden spots appear.)

Not the Kiss of Death

ONE OF THE best parts of having a long-running show was that the producers needed to keep adding fresh characters, which meant we got the opportunity to work with more great talents. Ali MacGraw came in at the same time that Rock Hudson joined the cast of *Dynasty*. The producers expected both to generate a lot of excitement and press.

I'd met Rock Hudson years before, when I was married to John Derek and did a guest spot on *McMillan & Wife*. Susan Saint James played Rock's wife on the show, but they brought me in as a way to test the character's moral fiber. His character passed with honors, but Rock decided to use the situation to play a joke on the director and crew—if I was game. Once I heard his plan, I couldn't resist.

We were filming inside a train, making for very cramped quarters, but perfect for his practical joke. Rock and I were alone in one of the little compartments waiting for the next scene. Just as the door opened, he threw me down on the pullout bed and kissed me for the longest time. The director and everyone else were so shocked they tried to back out and shut the door until they heard Rock and I finally burst out laughing. My God, could he kiss!

Rock and I got on famously, so over the years, we'd always be happy when we'd run into each other socially—like the time on Bunky's birthday, when Rock just happened to be at the same restaurant and joined the party. That was the night that Bunky laughed so hard she wet her pants. Truth. (Later, when I refused to let her sit on the leather seats of my precious Mercedes for the ride home, she simply stuck her naked rear end out the car window. Unfortunately, her dangling posterior soon attracted some young boys on Sunset Boulevard that thought we were soliciting them, so they started following us. When Bunky told me to "give them the slip," I turned a little too sharply and she nearly flew out the window. (The good news: we did lose the boys.)

After that night, I didn't see Rock again until he joined the cast of *Dynasty*. The producers wanted to spice things up by having Krystle and Blake cheat on each other, but John and I had agreed over the years to fight for our characters' integrity. The producers hired Ali MacGraw to entice Blake and Rock to tempt Krystle, saying the affairs were going to be fantastic for the ratings. John and I agreed it would be great—just not with our characters.

We found a compromise: I would be thrown from my horse in front of Rock's character and he'd rush over and take me into his arms. Then while Krystle was still dazed, Rock would passionately kiss her. It would happen at the very end of the episode, so everyone would think that he'd won her over at last.

However, when we actually shot the scene, instead of passionately kissing me, Rock just barely brushed his lips over mine and then backed away. The director yelled "Cut!" and we tried it again. It was exactly the same. So the director took Rock aside, explained the scene to him again and we tried it again, but Rock did exactly the same thing.

The director then tried asking me to help make the kiss more passionate. I explained that I couldn't without compromising Krystle's character. We shot the scene several more times, but always with the same lack of passion. They finally gave up and let us go home, but I knew the producers still weren't satisfied.

Weeks later, they decided that they were going to reshoot the scene, which they rarely ever did because it was so expensive. But this was the big season teaser, so we went back out on location and tried it again. And again, it was the same thing: Rock just wouldn't *really* kiss me.

I knew from my experience in the train compartment during my stint at *McMillan & Wife* how passionately Rock could kiss. Why Rock refused to kiss me the same way on *Dynasty* became painfully clear when the news broke that he had AIDS. In retrospect, it was incredibly touching how

Rock was a beautiful man inside and out.

hard he tried to protect me. No matter how much the director and producers pressed, he refused to put me at risk, because in those days so little was known about the disease.

When the truth about Rock's condition came out, it ignited a wildfire in the press. The cover of every tabloid and even some respectable magazines questioned whether Rock's kiss had given me AIDS.

The entire incident sparked a new awareness in me. It was tragic to see what fear can do to people. It became a media circus. In my heart, I knew Rock had protected me. I did what I could to support him. It all made me profoundly sad.

Later, after Rock passed, his good friend Elizabeth Taylor invited me to be a presenter at the launch of her HIV/AIDS foundation. That evening we had a chance to talk about what a remarkable man Rock Hudson had been.

Blondes *Do* Have More Fun

While I was doing *Dynasty*, unbeknownst to me, Clairol ran a contest to learn who America's favorite blonde was at the time. Lucky for me, it was me. Clairol turned out to be one of the most exceptional companies I've ever been associated with.

One of my responsibilities as the spokesperson for Ultress was to present the check from Clairol to the winner of the U.S. Open Women's Singles tennis tournament in New York. Every year, Clairol was generous enough to let me use their private jet and invite family and close friends. They even arranged for the hotel. It was a magical time for everyone who went on these trips. All anyone had to do was show up at the private airport on time—which was always a problem for my beloved agent, Greeny. One trip, knowing he would be late as usual, Bunky devised one of her infamous practical jokes to be played on Michael during the flight.

While everyone waited for Michael, Bunky briefed the group. She had bought and wrapped birthday gifts and made out cards for each of them to give to me. Now, it was August and my birthday isn't until November, but since we knew Michael relied on Bunky to tell him when it was my birthday and what to get me, we knew he'd fall for it.

Midway through the flight, after a sumptuous lunch, Bunky hatched her plan. As the candled cake was presented to me, everyone yelled "Surprise!" pulled out their gifts, and sang "Happy Birthday"—and they somehow managed not to crack up when they saw Michael's jaw drop. He, of course, was furious with Bunky for not telling him that it was my birthday.

We kept the charade going as long as we could, but eventually everyone started laughing, including Michael once he realized what was going on. Actually, he was so relieved he hadn't forgotten my birthday he nearly forgave Bunky. Nearly. As always, Michael vowed revenge, but took it like a good sport.

What he didn't know was that Bunky was not finished with the tricks on this trip. Not even close. Later, Bunky convinced the president of Clairol to stick Michael with the dinner check for over twenty of us at Le Cirque, one of the finest, most expensive restaurants in Manhattan. The shock on his face was so intense I couldn't stand it and had to end the joke sooner than Bunky wanted.

Strangely enough, Michael loves these games with Bunky. He knows she never wastes a drop of her devious genius on anyone unless she adores them. The harder Bunky plots against you, the more she loves you. So it is an honor to become a target in her laser sight. Clearly, Michael is *very* loved by her.

CHOCOLATE SOUFFLÉ PUDDING

Bunky thinks of Michael as a pit bull on the outside but soft inside. He loves chocolate, so here's a favorite I have cooked for him many times to match his sweet heart.

This soothing baked dessert combines a smooth custardy bottom layer with a very tender soufflélike top. It tastes like warm, soft, puffy brownies mixed up with chocolate custard sauce; this sums it up rather nicely, I think. Souffléd puddings are old-fashioned American desserts. In some old regional cookbooks they are called puffed puddings or just puffs. I appreciate Nancy Baggett for giving me this fabulous recipe from her book *The International Chocolate Cookbook*.

MAKES 6 TO 8 SERVINGS

1¾ cups heavy (whipping) cream

4½ ounces bittersweet (*NOT* sweetened) or semisweet chocolate, chopped into ¼ inch pieces

1 cup whole milk

6 tablespoons unsalted butter, slightly softened

⅔ cup packed light or dark brown sugar

1½ tablespoons unsweetened cocoa powder

1 large egg, plus 4 large egg yolks

⅓ cup all-purpose flour

2½ teaspoons vanilla extract

4 large egg whites, completely free of yolks

⅛ teaspoon salt

¼ cup granulated sugar

Lightly sweetened whipped cream for garnish (optional)

Position a rack in center of oven and preheat to 350°.

Generously grease a 2½-quart casserole or soufflé dish. Set out a baking pan large enough to hold the casserole.

In a medium saucepan over medium-high heat bring cream just to a boil. Immediately remove from heat. Pour ¼ cup cream over chocolate in a small deep bowl, stirring until chocolate partially melts and mixture is well blended. Stir in a ¼ cup more cream until chocolate completely melts and mixture is smooth. Stir chocolate mixture back into remaining cream until smoothly incorporated. Slowly stir milk into cream mixture until well blended and smooth.

In a large mixer bowl with mixer set on medium speed, beat butter and brown sugar for 2 or 3 minutes until very light and fluffy.

Beat in cocoa powder until well blended. One at a time, beat in egg and yolks. Beat in flour and vanilla just until smoothly incorporated.

168

Reduce mixer speed to low and slowly beat in chocolate mixture, scraping to bowl bottom to be sure mixture is thoroughly blended.

In a separate, completely grease-free mixer bowl with mixer set on medium speed, beat egg whites until frothy and opaque. Raise speed to high and continue beating until soft peaks just begin to form. Gradually beat in granulated sugar, continuing to beat until mixture stands in firm but not dry peaks. Add egg white mixture to chocolate mixture, folding with a wire whisk until evenly incorporated but not overmixed. Turn out mixture into soufflé dish. Immediately place dish in larger pan and transfer to oven. Add enough hot tap water to rise 1 inch up casserole sides.

Bake for 55 to 65 minutes or until mixture is set when tapped in center.

Remove large pan from oven; let soufflé dish stand in water bath for 10 to 15 minutes. Serve souffléd pudding immediately, spooned into bowls. Add a dollop of whipped cream, if desired. Alternatively, cover and refrigerate; rewarm in a low oven before serving. (The pudding will firm up and become brownie-like when chilled, and some people will like it that way.)

MOLTEN CHOCOLATE CAKES

This is my version of this classic dessert. As far as I am concerned you can never have too many for chocolate lovers.

MAKES 6 SERVINGS

15 tablespoons (1⅞ sticks) unsalted butter, plus additional for greasing

4 ounces bittersweet Ghirardelli chocolate

4 ounces semisweet Ghirardelli chocolate

1 teaspoon brewed coffee

4 large eggs, plus 4 large egg yolks, at room temperature

½ cup granulated sugar

1 teaspoon vanilla extract

7 tablespoons all-purpose flour, sifted

Preheat oven to 325°F. Butter and flour six (6-ounce) ramekins or six (6-ounce) glass Pyrex dishes. Place on a baking sheet lined with foil.

In a double boiler, melt the butter, chocolate, and coffee. Stir occasionally, until there is a smooth consistency. Remove from the heat and cool.

In a large bowl, beat the eggs, egg yolks, sugar, and vanilla with an electric mixer on medium speed for about 8 to 10 minutes.

Slowly add the flour on low speed, blending for 2 minutes.

Next add the cooled chocolate mixture and beat for 5 minutes more. The batter needs a lot of beating. This adds air and lightens the cake's texture.

Divide the mixture equally among the ramekins. Bake them in the middle of the oven until the edges are firm and the center jiggles slightly, for about 12 minutes. (If you want, you can refrigerate the ramekins and bake them later. But you will need to bake them 18 minutes instead of 12 if they are chilled from the refrigerator.) It is important the cakes cook for the correct amount of time, or they will be too molten or end up like brownies. Oven temperature varies, so check the cakes after 12 minutes, and if still too moist, cook another 2 minutes and check them again.

Remove from the oven and allow them to sit in the ramekins until ready to eat. They may sink a little.

Run a knife around the edge before inverting them onto individual serving plates. You may serve this with sweetened whipped cream.

Better Than a Van Gogh

OVER THE YEARS I've worked with some of the most talented artists in the industry. A few along the way also became dear friends, like Lon Bentley, a brilliant makeup artist (that I begrudgingly had to share with Tom Selleck and Robert Wagner).

Ironically, when Lon and I first met it was during *Tom Horn*, when Steve McQueen refused to let me wear any makeup. All Lon could do was make sure the gold cap I had to wear over my front tooth was in place; then he'd just slap my cheeks before each take to give me a bit of color. Thankfully, Lon's genius was unleashed later for my most glamorous *Dynasty* days as well as many other projects. We've remained dear friends ever since.

Another extraordinary artist that I admired and adored was Armando, who did my makeup and hair for all my magazine covers and the Clairol commercials. Armando and Bunky were kindred spirits, constantly clowning and conspiring to be sure *no one* was ever bored on the set.

We all became close friends over the years. Tragically, Armando contracted AIDS, but he did his best to fight the disease and tried to live as normal a life as possible. One of the main reasons I loved Clairol was because of the compassion they showed Armando. Knowing he was ill, they still allowed me to keep working with him. This was back when little was understood about the disease.

I know a lot about the prejudice and fear people had toward AIDS in those days. After the highly publicized kiss I shared with Rock Hudson, some of the actors on *Dynasty* wouldn't get near me and even close friends of mine were afraid to be around me.

I remember how poignant it was for Armando, especially toward the end. He was incredibly ill, hardly able to stand at times, but he was determined to be there for me. I, in turn, wanted him to know how much we loved and appreciated him. Clairol understood and allowed us to have our final days together. Who says that big companies can't have a heart?

Coyote Ugly:
In the Eye of the Beholder

I LOVE CATS. When I married John, we had six running around our Encino home. Since we lived up in the hills, I was always very protective and careful to bring my cats in every night because of the coyotes.

The same was true when I moved to my house in Beverly Hills: coyotes were notorious for killing small pets in the area. As cautious as I was, I still lost some of my beloved cats. Coyotes would often come running through our yards in packs at night, howling.

It is devastating enough to lose a pet, but it was tragic that we were losing so many animals to coyotes. It was particularly unnerving the way you'd know when they had their victim by the savage scream the pack would make.

One morning around five, while it was still dark, I was driving to the *Dynasty* set when suddenly I heard this bang on the side of my car. I instantly slammed on my brakes and looked in the rearview mirror. I saw a dark four-legged figure darting to the side of the road. I was horrified, thinking that I may have hit a dog. I quickly backed up but I couldn't see where it had disappeared.

Still believing it was a dog, I got out and found the creature hiding in some ivy. Frightened little eyes stared up at me; the eyes of a coyote lying there, hurt. Until that moment, I hated coyotes, or at least I thought I did. Looking into those eyes pierced my soul. She was so little, so vulnerable, that I knew I couldn't leave her there to die. But I didn't know what to do.

Fortunately I had my car phone, so I called my home security company, hoping they could dispatch a patrolman to help me. But at that hour all I got was an answering machine. The same happened when I tried calling animal rescue and my vet.

The sun was coming up and I knew I would hold up filming if I didn't leave right away. I've never been late for work in my life. I was out of options. When I tried to get a closer look at her she growled. I could see that she was as frightened as I was. So I did the only thing I could think of: I took off my coat and took a deep breath and threw it over the coyote. I scooped her up and rushed to my Jeep Wagoneer. I kept her wrapped in the coat, placed her in the back, and slammed the hatch.

As I drove toward the studio, desperate to find a veterinary hospital, I glimpsed movement in the rearview mirror and saw that the coyote was coming out from under the coat. Now I wasn't just upset, I was scared.

Just then, I saw a parked police car and quickly pulled up in front of it. I ran to it thinking, thank God, I can get help. I wasn't thinking about what I must have looked like when I started rambling through my tears about having a coyote in my car and that I was late for work. There were two officers, one male and one female, who looked at each other as if I was totally insane. The female officer followed me to my car and then nodded to her partner, "Yep, there really is a coyote back there."

My prayers were answered because she got in my car "to protect me" while I drove to the studio, with her partner following in the squad car.

When I arrived at the gate with my police escorts, needless to say, the security guard was surprised. But not nearly as surprised as John Forsythe, who'd also just pulled in.

I still wasn't sure what to do next. I couldn't leave the studio since I was scheduled to work all day. The officers said they were going off-duty shortly and they could take her to the nearest emergency animal hospital. I thanked them from the bottom of my heart and gave them a check for the vet.

Feeling hopeful, I went to the makeup department to see if they could work a miracle. Wouldn't you know, it was one of the few days Krystle didn't have a crying scene.

Later that afternoon, I heard from the vet that they couldn't save her. I felt a deep sadness—I couldn't forget the vulnerability in her eyes. There was so much more to her than just the predator.

At the end of the day, I went to have my wardrobe fitting with Nolan Miller. Rumors had spread quickly around the studio about my coming to work with the cops and a coyote. Nolan, noticing that I was emotionally struggling with it, said he was sorry to hear about what had happened and tried to cheer me up by saying, "I know we're having budget cuts, but really, Linda, you don't have to bag your own furs!" Through my tears, I could not stop laughing.

The famous Dynasty *staircase with Nolan Miller.*

I blessed that morning, and my encounter with the coyote. She gave me a greater understanding and compassion for something I thought I hated . . . that is, until I looked into her eyes. Now I see that predators are simply trying to survive . . . just like us.

Little did I know, my younger sister, Kat, would experience a similar revelation many decades later.

Every family usually has one special person that stands out from all the rest, and my beloved sister Kat is that special person in my family. Just a little over five feet tall, with a truly independent spirit, she's a petite and witty bundle of fire.

When my two nephews (Charlie's sons), Jimmy and Bruce, were four and five years old, Kat was only fifteen and a great built-in baby-sitter. She was a total hippy at the time, with her long black hair in ponytails on each side of her head, laced with feathers and beads. All of her jackets were leather, with long, beaded fringe, much like one Davy Crockett would have worn. My nephews thought she was the "coolest aunt and babysitter" and now in their fifties, they're still close to her. Charlie and I feel exactly the same way: we are truly blessed to have Kat as our sister.

The three of us are all animal lovers, but Kat loved her cats so much that when her last one passed, she couldn't face the heartbreak again.

Courtesy Kat Evenstad

Kat's coyote, Doug.

For the first time in her life, she didn't have a pet to care for.

Having gone through my own coyote experience, I couldn't have been more surprised when Kat sent me an e-mail titled "Breakfast With Doug," which featured a picture of a coyote having "breakfast" in her backyard. We had to laugh—she was feeding the enemy. Actually, not just feeding it, but providing a feast—often Doug dined on left-

Courtesy Kat Evenstad

My sister Kat and her fantastico *husband Al.*

overs I would have killed for. You see, my sister's husband, Al, is an exceptional cook, specializing in both Cuban and classic Spanish cuisine, having lived in both countries.

Al is my ideal brother-in-law, not only because I adore his cooking, but also because he adores my sister and all her nature-loving, wondrous eccentricities. I was thrilled when Kat fell in love with this wonderful man. For his paella, Al says getting the rice to the exact al dente point of cooking is the key. It may take a few tries to get it just right and it is easy to be discouraged when considering the expense of the ingredients. I think it is well worth the effort.

MARI-CARMEN-STYLE PAELLA

Mediterranean short-grain rice, such as Arborio, offers the ideal texture for classic paella. More pressing for authenticity is a paella pan—large, round, completely flat-bottomed. Al says a large skillet will make a rice and seafood dish but it won't be paella.

MAKES 6 SERVINGS

½ pound raw large shrimp (24 count to a pound)

4 cups seafood broth (chicken broth will work in a pinch)

¼ cup olive oil

1 medium green bell pepper, finely minced (about 1 cup)

1 medium yellow onion, finely minced (about 1 cup)

6 garlic cloves, minced

2 small tomatoes, peeled, seeded, and finely chopped

½ pound clams or mussels, beards removed

1 to 2 pinches saffron

Salt and pepper, to taste

2 cups Spanish short-grain rice (such as Arborio), unwashed

½ pound squid, bodies cut in ½-inch rings

½ to 1 pound firm-fleshed white fish (such as monkfish or halibut), cut in 1- to 1½-inch thick cubes

⅓ cup diced pimento (or ½ of a roasted red bell pepper, chopped), optional

Al's Aïoli, optional (page 180)

Peel and clean the shrimp. Set aside the shells for making the seafood broth richer.

Pour the fish broth into a medium saucepan over medium-high heat and add the shells of the shrimp. Bring to a boil and simmer until the shells turn pink, 5 to 7 minutes. Strain the broth with a fine sieve or coffee filter, discarding the solids. Pour the broth back into the saucepan and set aside.

Place a paella pan on a large burner on medium-low, and add the olive oil. Add the bell pepper, onion, garlic, and tomatoes to cook at medium-low heat until soft.

Bring the seafood broth to a boil and put in the clams or mussels; leave in the broth until they open. Remove the clams or mussels from the broth and set aside. Pour the broth into the paella pan and add the saffron, crumbling it between your fingers to release its fragrance. Add salt and pepper to taste.

Increase the heat and bring the liquid to a boil. Add the rice and stir to mix all ingredients. After the rice mixture has cooked for 5 minutes, add the shrimp, squid, fish, and clams or mussels, making sure to immerse them into the rice/broth mixture. Continue cooking uncovered for about 15 minutes, until the rice has absorbed the liquid. (Instead of cooking on the stovetop, you can put the pan into a 400°F oven, which I find allows for more even cooking.) Check the rice for perfect al dente texture to know when it is done—it should retain a hint of firmness in the center.

Let the paella sit for a few minutes prior to serving to help it set. If desired, add pimentos or a dollop of aïoli before serving.

AL'S AÏOLI

You will need an immersion blender (or standard blender) for this recipe.

- 2 to 3 garlic cloves, minced
- 1 whole egg plus 1 egg yolk, at room temperature
- ¼ teaspoon ground white pepper
- 2 to 3 teaspoons freshly squeezed lemon juice
- ¾ cup pure olive oil
- ¼ cup extra-virgin olive oil

Place the garlic, egg, egg yolk, salt, pepper, and lemon juice in the bottom of an immersion blender beaker. Blend for 5 seconds. Add the olive oils and, holding the blade against the bottom of the beaker, process until mixture begins to thicken, for about 30 seconds. Continue processing with a gentle up and down motion until the mixture is thick like mayonnaise.

My Heavenly Blue Angels

ONE OF THE executive producers of *Dynasty*, E. Duke Vincent, was a pilot with the Blue Angels. On the set, he'd tell stories about how exciting it was to fly the F/A-18s and what incredible machines they were. It sounded so thrilling that I said I wished I could experience it and, to my surprise, Duke told me he could arrange it.

Once all the guys on the set learned I was going to be flying with the Blue Angels they started warning me that it wasn't as simple as I imagined. They also warned me not to eat or drink anything the night before. It turned out to be great advice. As Bunky and I drove out to the El Toro air base early in the morning, I was already flying high with excitement. Bunky, on the other hand, was a little more apprehensive, especially when we stood on the tarmac looking up at the magnificent aircraft. Then when they presented me with my very own fireproof suit, Bunky really started to get nervous.

They introduced me to a very cute and charming pilot, whose nickname was "Hollywood" because he was the one that always flew the celebrities in a unique two-seater jet. After strapping me in so tight that I could hardly breathe, I was shown the air sickness bags directly in front of me to be used "just in case." Before I could finish waving through the window to Bunky, the plane shot straight into the air and up into the clouds. As Bunky put it, "They were out of sight in the blink of an eye." And that's when she started praying in earnest.

When we leveled off and I looked out, the ocean gleaming below us, I started to cry—it was so amazingly beautiful. I felt so fortunate to be having this truly unique experience with one of the elite Blue Angels. When he offered to give me either a "gentle ride" or "the works," I told him, "This will probably be the only time I'll ever get to do this, so give me all you've got."

Clueless!

182

I couldn't see his face when he asked if I was sure, but his tone spoke volumes. He said: "Okay. But I'll ask you again after each demonstration."

The first few rolls, flips, spins, and dives were really exciting and I was starting to think the experience was going to be a breeze, but then I quickly realized he was saving the hardest stuff to stomach for last.

As our speed increased with every flip and spin, Hollywood reminded me where the sickness bags were. Because he had a mirror in place to see if his passenger was turning green, he began making the pauses between demonstrations a bit longer each time. I could see his shoulders going up and down as he fought not to laugh at the absurdity of me, gagging, all the while insisting that I was fine. I just didn't want to miss any part of the experience. I refused to surrender, even when he asked me if I'd like to know what g-force feels like.

We've all seen it in the movies: the person's face stretched ridiculously like they are in a wind tunnel. But I had no idea that I would lose my peripheral vision and then black out. A second later when I came to, Hollywood explained what had happened and I wondered how he had been able to remain conscious. "You did, didn't you?" I asked. He laughed and explained that they go through months of training to acclimate their bodies to the force.

For the grand finale on the way back to the airport, Hollywood offered me a "simulated aircraft carrier landing." I just couldn't stop myself from agreeing. So, a moment later, he rolled the plane over, pulled the nose up hard, and the jet stopped immediately on the landing field. Talk about stopping on a dime. My chest slammed against the seat belts, while my head and my neck went places they'd never been before. If that was just a simulation, I can honestly say I never want to land on an aircraft carrier.

At last we were down and I could find a quiet bathroom, feeling proud I'd never had to reach for the bag. But to my horror, the entire Blue Angel squad was standing with Bunky, waiting to have their pictures taken with me, and *Entertainment Tonight* was already filming as I shakily climbed down from the plane.

Courtesy Blue Angels

Excited to be flying with the Blue Angels.

I don't remember the interview, but I do remember the minute it was all over telling Bunky to get in the car fast. I drove off the base at full speed. As soon as we were out of sight, I got out and handed Bunky the keys, collapsing into the backseat. She drove me immediately to the nearest chiropractor.

A few days later, I was still green, which Bunky informed me was not my best color. Even so, it was an amazing experience and, pea green or not, I wouldn't have missed a moment of it.

The Weight of the World

During the height of *Dynasty's* success, the network decided we should do a commercial to promote the upcoming season. They wanted it to be very romantic and sexy: Blake carrying Krystle up the grand staircase to the bedroom, a la *Gone with the Wind*. I loved doing those scenes.

John and I had unusually late calls that day, coming in around eleven in the morning, instead of our usual six o'clock. We didn't bother to change and were still in jeans, looking less than Carrington-like.

During rehearsal, John dramatically swept me into his arms and up the length of the stairs, with the cameras following and the lighting crew working their magic. This was going to be a piece of cake. So we broke for lunch, agreeing to be back on the set "camera ready," that is, in tux and gown.

For this commercial, Nolan Miller had made me an exquisite beaded gown, which was so beautiful John applauded when I arrived on the set. John was always so thoughtful and kind in moments like this.

The director yelled "Roll camera," then "Action!" John and I exchanged a couple of romantic lines, and then John dramatically picked me up—and promptly fell to his knees, sending me rolling to the floor. "Cut!"

Everyone was silent on the set as John looked at me in horror for a long beat, then asked, "What did you eat for lunch?"

All I could do was laugh. I had no idea why he'd been able to carry me around half the morning with no problem, but suddenly was acting like I weighed a ton. Well, not exactly a ton—but I was now wearing at least twenty-five pounds of hand-stitched beads on my gown.

Once we figured it out, the whole set burst out laughing and John vowed never again to do a scene like that before consulting with Nolan

Carrying on with John

on my wardrobe. Needless to say, I changed into a lighter beaded dress so we could complete the scene.

The moral of the story: never attempt any romantic carryings-on in a beaded gown.

GREAT AND SIMPLE CHEESE SOUFFLÉ

If you are usually afraid of attempting a soufflé, don't be afraid of this one. This is unlike any other cheese soufflé, because in this one you don't need to beat egg whites and fold them in. You can even assemble it up to two hours ahead and bake it just before serving. Serve immediately as, like all soufflés, it will fall. Believe it or not this is a low carbohydrate recipe.

MAKES 6 SERVINGS

1 tablespoon unsalted butter

6 eggs

½ cup heavy cream

½ cup grated Parmesan cheese

1 teaspoon prepared yellow mustard

¼ to ½ teaspoon kosher salt, or ¼ teaspoon iodized salt

¼ teaspoon pepper

1 teaspoon hot sauce

½ pound cheddar cheese, cut into large chunks

11 ounces cream cheese, cut into large chunks

Preheat oven to 375°F. Grease a 6-cup soufflé dish with the butter.

In a food processor, combine the eggs, cream, Parmesan, mustard, salt, pepper, and hot sauce. Blend until smooth.

Add cheddar and cream cheese chunks and pulse to blend until completely smooth and all ingredients, especially the cream cheese, are incorporated; this may take up to 5 minutes. Scrape the sides and pulse again to make sure it is well blended.

Pour into soufflé dish and bake for 50 to 60 minutes.

A Taste of a Real-Life Dynasty

MY DIVORCE FROM my second husband Stan was very amicable, so it wasn't necessary to divide up our friends; fortunately, a couple of other friends of ours had a friendly split as well: Tina Sinatra and Richard Cohen. So, years later, when Richard and I decided to start dating, it wasn't awkward at all. I'd known him quite a while and knew that his reputation for being "one of the good guys" was absolutely justified.

Thankfully, I was finally ready for a man who was both loyal and ethical. Richard was a truly wonderful man and I loved being with him, so we decided to try living together.

Although our houses were only minutes apart, Richard lived in a very different world. His was as opulent as a real-life *Dynasty*, but without all the drama and the angry ex.

Courtesy Linda Evans

A snug fit.

189

Two of the passions that Richard and I shared were art and great food. So Richard would take me to Paris, where we'd start off the trip with dinner at the House of Caviar, having beluga and blinis. Then we'd visit endless galleries while Richard began teaching me how to be a savvy art collector.

Coming up roses.

Richard loved life and lived it to the fullest, and in many ways he was every woman's dream. He was charming, bright, funny, athletic, and very romantic. He put a lot of thought into the gifts he gave me, and it was beautiful to see how much joy he got from giving. It wasn't uncommon to get into bed at night and jump with surprise when my foot touched something unexpected like a small painting, diamond necklace, or ruby bracelet. Richard was extremely generous and sharing with those he loved.

His warm and beautiful home was always filled with friends and family: by day for tennis and by night for movie screenings and dinners. His dear friends became my friends and we shared many amazing times laughing and cooking together.

190

Cooking up fun with Louis Jordan.

When we met, Richard already had a great chef working for him, so I felt privileged to share the kitchen with Andrew.

The Royal Tasters: Bridget, Louis Jordan,
me, Richard, Sidney Poitier.

I'm not sure Nena always agreed, but we both learned a great deal from him.

"Ritzy" Business

WHILE I WAS with Richard, I had to go to Madrid for work, so Bunky and Armando came with us. We stayed at the Ritz, a very old, classically elegant hotel. They gave us the most enormous, extraordinary two-bedroom suite any of us had ever seen. Richard and I stayed in one bedroom; Bunky stayed in the second bedroom, which felt like a half a block away from ours—that's how big the suite was. Armando had yet another room next door to Bunky, but they weren't adjoining.

Early every morning, still in our pajamas, we'd sneak down the hall to Armando's room to get hair and makeup done, hoping not to run into anyone. Regardless of our efforts to be invisible, the housekeepers walked in and caught us in our pajamas with Armando. Thinking we were "together," they started turning down both beds in his room. We had a good laugh over it.

One day, Bunky was in her bedroom watching TV when she heard knocking. She went to the door but there was no one there. She suddenly thought she heard Armando's voice inside her room, but she knew that was impossible. But then she heard it again, "Bunky over here!" Completely perplexed, she followed his voice to a big antique armoire against the wall. She opened it to find a grinning Armando standing in her closet. He'd obviously discovered some ancient secret passage used by wealthy nobles for secrets trysts, back in the day. The good news was we didn't have to worry about being seen in the halls in our pajamas anymore.

One evening, after a very long day of work, we decided to have a casual dinner in our suite. Richard and I just wanted to kick back in our jeans, so needless to say we were floored when Bunky suddenly sauntered

Bunky in Madrid—Ole!

out of her bedroom, looking like she'd borrowed one of Jean Harlow's silk nightgowns from the 1930s. While we just stared, she moved to the fruit bowl and selected two oranges to add to her already ample cleavage. But given the Harlow-esque style of the gown, they had a life of their own, swinging around, not always in the same direction.

While Richard and I were doubled over laughing, our dinner was brought in by a parade of waiters, all in black tie, each carrying a silver-domed dish (clearly sent to make sure "Mrs. Carrington" was well taken care of).

So there we were, Richard and I in our jeans and Bunky in her gown with the two oranges (which she propped, one at a time, on the table), while the poor waiters pretended not to stare.

Richard was laughing so hard he had tears running down his face as the waiters served us and then politely departed—no doubt to report that Mrs. Carrington and her friends weren't exactly what they had been expecting.

It was a truly outrageous evening. I seem to have them when I visit Spain. I love Spanish food, particularly their pork dishes. I remember during another trip to Madrid, I tried to order one of my favorites, but this time it came to the table with the hoof attached. Clearly my Spanish needs help. Somehow, I managed to work my way around it and still enjoy the meal.

Real Princes among Men

ONE OF THE great joys of doing *Dynasty* was all the amazing invitations we'd receive. Obviously there wasn't enough time to accept them all, but one year we got one that was irresistible and, better yet, for a worthy cause. Prince Charles was participating in a polo match and luncheon to benefit a wonderful charity. Everything about the event sounded fabulous.

John Forsythe and I were asked to each donate a personal item for the auction. I decided to give one of the jackets John and I had made for the cast and crew for Christmas the previous year. They were very simple black jackets with *Dynasty* written in red on them, but everyone loved them.

So John and Julie and Richard and I flew to England. It was the first time I had the pleasure of meeting Prince Charles, whom I found to be charismatic and a real Prince Charming, as well as a heck of a polo player.

It was a magical day. The polo was thrilling and luncheon wonderful. Then it was time to begin the auction and I suddenly realized how emotionally attached I was to that silly, sweet little *Dynasty* jacket of mine. But I thought it would be in bad taste to bid on my own donation, so I just reminded myself it was going to a good cause.

The bidding began and very quickly it climbed higher and higher, which made me feel better knowing it was making a lot of money for the charity. But then I saw Richard raise his hand and join in the bidding. I was deeply touched when I realized he was trying to get it back for me. But then the bidding went so high it was outrageous and I asked him to stop, but the man was on a mission. It escalated into a bidding war, because across the room it appeared that someone was equally passionate to have my jacket at any cost. We couldn't see who was bidding against us, so of course the other bidder couldn't see Richard either. This was lucky for the charity, because the other dear heart trying to win my jacket back for me was John.

Everybody wins—me the most!

A Royal Welcome

ONE OF THE most memorable trips was when I was invited to have tea with the queen. But when I arrived, it wasn't exactly how I imagined it would be, since there were about a hundred other people besides the queen and me. When I entered the room, the orchestra started playing the *Dynasty* theme. Suddenly, everyone, including the Queen of England, stopped and turned to stare at me. I was so caught off guard and so embarrassed, I felt like diving under the nearest table to hide—but it was the queen's table, so that really wasn't an option.

Greeting her Majesty the Queen.

WARM BUTTERNUT SQUASH SALAD

During my stay in London to visit the queen, I discovered a wonderful butternut squash salad. My friend Bunky loves butternut squash, so when I came home, I decided to try out my own version of this yummy dish. After testing and refining, I have finally come up with a salad I love.

MAKES 6 SERVINGS

1 cup Marcona almonds (these are my favorite but any almonds will do)

3 tablespoons olive oil

Kosher salt and black pepper

½ teaspoon paprika

1 large butternut squash (about 1 pound), peeled, cleaned, and
   cut into ¾-inch cubes

1 small red onion, finely diced (about ½ cup)

¼ teaspoon seasoned salt (I use Lawry's Garlic Salt)

¼ teaspoon ground cumin

¼ teaspoon onion powder

¼ teaspoon garlic powder

Pinch of cayenne, to taste

7 cups mixed salad greens

¾ to 1 cup crumbled feta cheese

DRESSING (I LIKE TO MAKE A LOT, USE TO TASTE)

2 tablespoons extra-virgin olive oil

1 tablespoon whole-grain mustard

2 tablespoons freshly squeezed lemon juice

4 tablespoons pure grade A maple syrup

Preheat oven to 400°F.

Toss the almonds with a tablespoon of olive oil, 1 teaspoon of salt, and paprika. Spread on a baking sheet and bake for approximately 5 minutes. Keep a close eye on the nuts as they burn easily; when toasted, remove from the oven and set aside to cool.

Put the squash and onion in a large mixing bowl. Drizzle with 2 tablespoons of olive oil, and toss with the seasoned salt, cumin, onion and garlic powder, and cayenne. When ready to cook, place in a baking dish, sprinkle lightly with salt and pepper, and roast for about 15 to 20 minutes, just until tender. Stir halfway through for even browning.

Whisk the dressing ingredients together in a small bowl. Put the salad greens in a large bowl, add dressing to taste, and toss well.

Divide greens between six plates. Top with squash, almonds, and feta cheese. Serve immediately.

Dynasty Fans Even in the Vatican?

DURING MY VISIT to the Vatican, I was introduced to countless priests and other clergy, all very excited about meeting "Krystle." I was stunned that they actually watched *Dynasty*. I remember thinking: I sure hope the pope doesn't watch it, too. I mean he must have better things to do . . . right?

Touched by the Pope.

Of course, being raised catholic, the pope had always been held in high esteem by my mom. His Holiness was one step away from God: next level you were in heaven.

200

As is always the case, thousands of people gathered outside the Vatican to see the pope. I was part of a small group that was going to meet him personally. I was with my friend Bridget Hedison, and the two of us could see Pope Paul moving along the line toward us, stopping to talk to people. As he got closer, I remember my heart was beating a little faster and I was thinking, *Oh please don't call me Krystle.*

The pope took my hand, smiled sweetly, and asked: "Buenos Aires?"

I replied that I was an American and he smiled and nodded while I beamed inside, so relieved that His Holiness had no idea who I was.

The Price of Fame

DURING THE *DYNASTY* years, I rarely had free time during the day to go to a restaurant. Our schedule was so intense that when I had time off, I would be doing fittings with Nolan Miller, interviews, photo shoots, or studying my lines for the next day and often the next week's show as well. I've always been in awe of people that have the extraordinary ability to memorize lines, in what seems like a matter of minutes.

Any chance I got, I'd go to my favorite restaurant, La Scala, for lunch and have their famous Leon Chopped Salad. I love this salad so much that when I did a guest appearance on the *North and South, Book II* miniseries, Michael was so excited that I was the highest paid female to date for a one-day shoot that he offered to bring me lunch on the set from any restaurant anywhere to celebrate. Without batting an eye, I blurted out "La Scala's chopped salad." Now if Bunky had been choosing, she'd have probably made Greeny order from Maxim's in Paris. But I still prefer the "Leon's Chopped."

Aside from running into dear friends like Dani Janssen, Polly Bergen, and Suzanne Pleshette, what was so great about this restaurant was that the staff was very respectful of everyone's privacy. We could just go there and relax with friends. However, one day while Bunky and I were eating our chopped salads with great joy, we sensed a presence and discovered a man standing uncomfortably close, just staring at me.

When I looked up and made eye contact, he asked, "Linda, don't you remember me?"

I said I was sorry but I didn't, and then he blurted out, "But I'm your husband!"

Bunky and I exchanged a knowing look, because she kept a special file for fans like this gentleman. He sincerely believed we were married. Others were far more frightening, to the point that the FBI had to become involved. As a result, Bunky would get a little unnerved in these kinds of situations.

I'm never sure what to say, but this time I was really thrown, because my "husband" began drooling—literally making a pool on the table. We were both praying the maître d' would come to our rescue, which she finally did, escorting the man out the front door. Bunky and I slipped out the back, deciding to do our errands first, then maybe come back for our salads later.

As we picked up things from several stores in Beverly Hills, I was greeted by salespeople, all cheerfully telling me that my husband had just been there looking for me. After four or five stores we decided to call it quits and head for home.

Throughout my career, fortunately, 99.9 percent of my fans have been extraordinary and supportive. I believe part of it is because the characters I have played resonate with the best part of us as people.

Thrilled to be reaching back.

Unfortunately for John, there was a point on the show when the writers had Blake mistreating Kystle. John really wanted our characters to make up soon, because it seemed every weekend when he'd travel for a tennis tournament or the horse races, he'd come across irate Krystle fans. At one point, he was even attacked by a little old lady in a hairnet, just like Ruth Buzzi on *Laugh-In*. She got right in his face and shouted, "You treat your wife terribly!" Then she chased him through the airport, hitting him with her purse.

My Spiritual Journey
Leads Me Home

WHEN I WAS married to John Derek, I did a guest spot on *McCloud* with Dennis Weaver. What few people knew about Dennis is that he was a lay minister at the Self-Realization Fellowship. While we were working together, he invited me to one of their Sunday morning services. I was very moved by Dennis's sermon, which I learned was based on the teachings of Paramahansa Yogananda. Later, Dennis gave me the book that he said had changed his life, called *Autobiography of a Yogi*.

Because of Dennis I took the first step in what would become a lifelong spiritual journey. After spending years studying at the Self-Realization Fellowship in Malibu, I went on to learn all I could from books and other teachers, like Ernest Holmes, Eckhart Tolle, Abraham-Hicks, Byron Katie, and Patricia Sun. I have always enjoyed hearing other people's perspectives. I believe there are many ways to arrive at the same empowered place.

One day, a friend gave me a book with a plain white cover. Inside was a passage that touched a chord in me. It said: "We are all divine beings." It spoke of the absolute equality for men and women and resonated for me on so many levels. But mostly it confirmed my belief that God is in everyone and everything and that God is unconditionally loving.

This white book was my introduction to Ramtha, who teaches that each and every one of us create our reality. Students of Ramtha are initiated into this philosophy through disciplines so that it becomes their personal truth. Ramtha is channeled by a remarkable woman named JZ Knight.

With my dear friend JZ on her birthday.

Courtesy Linda Evans

When I heard Ramtha would be speaking in Yucca Valley, California, one Sunday, I invited my friend Linda McCallum to come with me. That day, Ramtha touched my soul with his words. I wanted to know more. I traveled up to Washington State, where JZ lived and did most of the Ramtha teachings at the school called RSE.

When I first meet JZ I loved how down to earth and simple she was. Our first conversation was about baking and pies! I connected to her instantly. I find it fascinating that you can meet someone for the first time and feel as though you've known her forever. Bunky was like a mom to me, JZ a sister. I have a deep respect for her, not just for her courage to channel, but because she is one of the most loving and generous people I know.

I'd never been to the Pacific Northwest and I fell in love with its extraordinary natural beauty. I'd been thinking about having a getaway home and I knew I'd found the perfect setting. I discovered an old Italian villa for sale on a private lake. When I walked into the kitchen and saw that it had five ovens and two dishwashers, I knew I had come home.

With all the madness surrounding *Dynasty*, Villa Madera was the perfect refuge, even if it was only for a quick weekend here and there. It was never my intention to move to the Pacific Northwest full time. I still had a beautiful home in Beverly Hills, but I found myself loving the nature and the privacy of Washington State.

My beautiful Villa Madera.

Most everyone thought I was crazy "escaping" Beverly Hills for the "Land of Rain." John Forsythe used to call me just to ask if the sun had come out yet.

View of the terrace from the lake.

JZ'S AWARD-WINNING LEMON MERINGUE PIE

No kidding, JZ really did win an award for this pie when she was young. And I have to say it is the best I've had in my life.

MAKES 1 (9-INCH) PIE, SERVING 8

---

4 eggs, separated, yolks slightly beaten

¼ teaspoon cream of tartar

2½ cups granulated sugar

¾ teaspoon vanilla extract

½ cup cornstarch

4 tablespoons (½ stick) unsalted butter

2 teaspoons grated lemon peel

⅔ cup freshly squeezed lemon juice

1 or 2 drops yellow food coloring

1 9-inch baked pie shell (page 209)

Preheat oven to 400°F.

Make the meringue first: Beat egg whites and cream of tartar until frothy. Beat in ½ cup of sugar, 1 tablespoon at a time. Continue beating until stiff and glossy; do not under beat. Beat in vanilla. Reserve.

To make the filling, blend the remaining 2 cups of sugar and the cornstarch in a saucepan. Gradually stir in 2 cups of water. Cook, stirring constantly, over medium heat until mixture thickens and comes to a boil. Boil 1 minute, stirring. Gradually stir at least half the sugar mixture into the egg yolks, then blend all of the egg yolk mixture back into the sugar mixture in the pan. Boil and stir for 2 more minutes. Remove from the heat; stir in butter, lemon peel, juice, and food coloring. Immediately pour into the baked pie shell.

Heap meringue on the hot pie filling; spread over the filling, carefully sealing the meringue onto the edge of the crust to prevent shrinking or weeping. There will be extra filling and meringue for your own enjoyment.

Bake about 10 minutes, or until delicately browned. Cool the pie away from any draft.

JZ'S CLASSIC CRUST

MAKES A SINGLE 9-INCH PIE BOTTOM CRUST

1 cup all-purpose flour

½ teaspoon salt

4 tablespoons (½ stick) butter-flavored shortening, chilled,
    cut into ½-inch cubes

4 to 6 tablespoons water, ice cold

In a chilled mixing bowl, blend flour and salt. Cut the chilled cubes of butter-flavored shortening into the mixture using a pastry blender, until the mixture resembles course pea-size crumbs. Sprinkle half the iced water over the mixture and mix gently with a fork. Add additional tablespoons of iced water one at a time, until the dough holds together.

Quickly mold the dough into a ball, then flatten into a disk. Wrap in plastic wrap and refrigerate for at least 30 minutes.

Preheat the oven to 450°F.

Place the dough disk on a lightly floured surface and, with a rolling pin, roll dough outward from the center into a circle 2 inches wider than the pie plate. Gently ease the crust into the pie plate. Fold the edges under and crimp onto the edge of the pie plate.

Bake for 20 minutes or until a light golden brown. Remove from the oven and cool for 30 minutes.

March on the Capital

SHORTLY AFTER I purchased Villa Madera, a friend told me she'd uncovered plans to dump sludge next to a pristine river where the dwindling salmon spawn. She asked if I could help bring this potential disaster to the public's eye. So, JZ, I, and a group of our friends marched together on the state capital with hundreds of caring protesters.

Not only did we win the day, but also the Reagan Administration, having heard about the event, thought I'd be the perfect spokesperson for the president's environmental program, Take Pride in America. It

Courtesy of the Ronald Reagan Library

Dear Linda – Every good wish, our appreciation and Warmest Regard.

Nancy & Ronald Reagan

John and I hosting the gala for the Reagans at the Ford Theater.

was such a pleasure for me to meet the thousands of Americans that took part in the program over the years—beautiful, caring people who volunteered to help clean up our rivers, parks, and cities.

Take Pride in America was such a success that the Bush administration kept it alive for another four years. Sadly, and quite surprisingly, the so-called environmental administration of Clinton and Gore decided to dismantle it because "it was a Republican program." I tried telling them that the environment isn't a Republican or a Democrat (which and, by the way, I happen to be), but they just didn't care.

Taking Pride in America with President Bush.

It's sad that even as far back as that, partisan politics have created more harm than good. Here they were calling themselves the "Environmental Group," but only supported programs they personally implemented. I'm thrilled about all the great work that Al Gore has recently done on behalf of climate change; it's just sad that such a worthy project had to be shelved more than a decade ago, when it could have done so much good if given a chance.

CRAB AND LOBSTER CAKES WITH MUSTARD BEURRE BLANC

When I was in Washington, D.C., I fell in love with the crab cakes they made in the restaurant of the hotel where I stayed. When the chef found out how much I loved them, and how I also liked to cook, he invited me into the kitchen to watch him make them. What a wonderful experience that was! Through the years, with much trial and error, I think I finally came up with my winning version, which I serve with a creamy wine, shallot, and mustard sauce. I hope you like them, too!

MAKES 6 TO 8 SERVINGS

1 pound scallops

½ pound lump crabmeat

2 egg whites (plus 1 egg yolk, if mixture is too thin)

1 to 2 tablespoons heavy cream

½ pound cooked lobster meat; cut into small chunks (I use the much less expensive slipper lobster tails, ¾-pound uncooked to yield this much meat, see Note on page 214)

1½ to 2 cups panko breadcrumbs

¾ cup clarified unsalted butter (page 29)

Salmon caviar, optional

Chopped chives, optional

FOR THE SAUCE

¾ cup dry white wine

¼ cup white wine vinegar

2 tablespoons minced shallot

2 tablespoons heavy cream

1 pound unsalted butter, chilled, cut into small pieces

2 teaspoons whole-grain mustard (I prefer Pommery), or to taste,
   at room temperature

Pat dry the scallops. Pick through the crab to take out any shells.

Pulse the scallops in a food processor until finely chopped. Add egg whites and blend. (Only add the egg yolk if the mixture appears runny at this point.) With the machine running, slowly pour in the 1 to 2 tablespoons cream and blend until it has the consistency of thick mayonnaise. Pour into a bowl and fold in the crab and lobster meat.

Preheat the oven to 180°F.

Place the panko breadcrumbs on a large plate. Take a portion of the crab/lobster mixture with a ladle, enough to form a 3-inch crab cake (this mixture will not be stiff). Gently place the mixture on top of the panko breadcrumbs. With your hands, form it into a round cake and coat on the top and sides with the breadcrumbs, gently pressing the panko to adhere to the cakes. Place the coated cakes on a clean plate until they have all been formed and breaded.

Add a few tablespoons of clarified butter to a nonstick skillet over medium heat and sauté the cakes in batches, adding a little more butter as needed, until brown on both sides, 2 to 3 minutes altogether. Keep finished cakes warm on a cookie sheet in the oven.

To make the sauce, put the wine, vinegar, and shallots in a heavy-bottomed, medium saucepan over medium heat. Simmer until reduced to about 1½ tablespoons. Add the cream and reduce slightly as well. Remove the pan from the heat, and slowly add the chilled butter, one piece at a time, whisking constantly. If you need more heat for the butter to soften, hold the pan briefly over *very* low heat. Never let the butter melt completely or the sauce will separate. (If the sauce starts to separate, take it off the heat and let the warmth of the sauce soften the butter. You may have to repeat the process of heating and cooling so sauce does not separate.) Stir in the mustard to your taste.

Place a little sauce on each plate and place the crab cake on top.

Serve the sauce and the crab cakes immediately. If you must wait, hold the sauce over water that's just warm enough to keep the butter from separating.

Note: If you are using the slipper tail lobsters for the lobster meat, put them in a small frying pan with 1 tablespoon of melted butter and cook for a few minutes. Put on a plate lined with paper towels and pat dry. Three-quarters of a pound will cook down to half a pound of lobster. The pieces of meat will be perfect in size, so you do not need to cut them.

There's a Bunky Loose
in the White House

IT WAS LIKE a fairy tale to be invited to the White House for the first time, though I'm sure you can understand why I was nervous about taking Bunky with me to meet President and Mrs. Reagan. The way Bunky tells it, I threatened her within an inch of her life to behave. I probably did, but I also knew it wouldn't stop her if she'd made up her mind to do something outrageous.

At the White House, while the Marines were escorting us to the Blue Room, I kept asking Bunky what she was going to say to the President when they met. But all the little brat would say is: "I'm not gonna tell ya."

Off to meet the President!

215

Meanwhile, Julie Forsythe was the first in line. John and Julie knew the Reagans very well. I followed John and, as always, the President and Nancy could not have been more charming.

And then came Ms. Bunky, who looked quite elegant in a lovely black dress. I had to keep moving along with the reception line, so I couldn't hear, but I could see her chatting away with President Reagan, who suddenly lit up at something she said and took hold of her hand. I thought, "What in the world?"

Turns out, Bunky attended the church where Ronald Reagan and Nancy were married and she had a personal message from the pastor for the president. Of course if she'd just told me that I could have relaxed. But where's the fun in that?

Later that evening, the Marine Band played while we had cocktails, and I finally relaxed and felt safe. Bunky had behaved.

But then I noticed Bunky suddenly staring across the crowded room at a man dressed like Count Dracula in a long black cape. Oh no! It was Dom DeLuise, and he was staring right back at Bunky, through a sea of people. The two wild and crazies had somehow managed to spot each other and he was now weaving his way toward her like he was waltzing on air.

Dom grabbed Bunky's hand and kissed it while asking breathlessly, "Who are you?"

Without missing a beat, Bunky replied, "I am the Countess De La Valley." (Bunky was one of the original Valley girls.)

Dom said, "I knew it!"

That did it. Dom and Bunky got on a roll, joking and laughing so much that soon they were surrounded, everyone drawn to their madness. They were the hit of the party. And I am happy to report I was invited back to the White House many, many times—with Bunky. Although on our next trip, Bunky was seated next to the head of the CIA. *Hmm.*

A Time for Change

For several reasons, I began questioning everything in my life around the end of the 1980s. *Dynasty* had given me tremendous gifts on every level, and I was grateful for each and every one of them. I had everything you can have that people think will make you happy. But I wasn't. Something was still missing. There were answers to things I wanted to know, but I couldn't find them. It was amazing: I had fame, fortune, and the love of people all around the world, and yet, I was unfulfilled.

I remember at the height of the success of *Dynasty* reflecting on my life as I sat in the back of a limo holding my fifth People's Choice award. I was accomplishing my goal, which was to have a career and to be self-sufficient. I thought, "Take a moment to bask in the sweetness of it." That moment was followed by a louder voice in my head. "Is this all there is?"

One of the wonderful things about getting your dream is you can finally let go of it for something new.

By the ninth year of *Dynasty*, in spite of all its blessings, I longed to be a regular person again. I wanted to take out the trash, go to the supermarket, and walk along the beach without being recognized. I didn't want to have to live up to people's expectations of me. I wasn't one of the ten most beautiful women in the world, like *Harper's Bazaar* said year after year. I was just fortunate enough to have a team of talented people assisting me with that image every day.

I made the decision to leave the show. Esther and Richard Shapiro, the creators of *Dynasty*, and Aaron Spelling gave me their blessings. I was an emotional mess my last day of filming. My makeup man had to use all of his Kleenex and get more. I couldn't stop crying. I would miss my *Dynasty* family, but it was time to go.

Hard changes were everywhere. Everyone I knew agreed that Richard was the greatest guy I'd ever known. So why didn't I want to settle down with him and live happily ever after? Even I thought I was crazy to be thinking about giving him up. I kept trying to figure out what was wrong with me. Then one day I realized I loved Richard with all my heart, but, cliché as it might sound, I wasn't *in love*. It was hard to explain why *being in love*, not *just loving*, was so important to me. It was an outrageous dilemma. But once I understood it, I couldn't stay with him.

So one day, Nena and the cats and I moved back home to my old house in Beverly Hills. For a very long time I wondered if I'd made the biggest mistake of my life. But then one day, I opened the door to find true love staring me in the face and God, was I happy to be free to embrace it.

Music to My Life

ONE OF THE things I love about the Ramtha retreats is the music they play to help us focus. I'll never forget one particular event when they played a magnificent piece of music, like nothing I'd ever heard before. It had a classical elegance and yet the energy was stunning. Everyone in the room was so moved by the passion of the piece, we all wanted to know who this new composer was.

He was just starting out and there wasn't a lot of information about him. Someone told me they thought he was Asian. Since his album cover didn't have a clear picture, I just assumed it was true.

Given the extraordinary response to his music at the retreats, JZ wanted to find out if he would consider coming in person. I was elected to make the call and his manager informed me that he was in his studio, immersed in creating a new album. He promised I would hear from him in a few weeks when he came out of seclusion.

When he called three weeks later, I was at Villa Madera. We had a great conversation and decided that we'd try to get together the next time I was in LA.

Between our busy schedules, the only time we could meet turned out to be a half an hour before I had to leave for the airport. I was rushing to pack and almost forgot that we had made an appointment, until Bunky told me that the music man was at the gate, but I better make it quick so we didn't miss the plane.

Now, I had spoken to him on the phone and learned that the name, Yanni, is Greek, not Asian, but I still had no idea what he looked like.

So, when I opened the door, I was stunned. I couldn't speak. I don't know what I had been expecting, but it wasn't the man I found standing there.

My mind exploded in a million directions. I couldn't believe my eyes. I loved everything about him. I wanted to slap him and say, "Where have you been all my life!" I was overwhelmed by the moment. I'm not sure how we ended up sitting on the couch talking. What I do remember is how upset I was every time Bunky came in to remind me that I had to leave for the airport.

Finally, Bunky had to walk us both to the door to get us to say goodbye. As he was leaving, I just stood there lost in thought, until Bunky turned to me and said, "Great ass." Before I could respond, the driver arrived to take us to the airport.

Later, when we finally settled down on the plane, Bunky noticed I was unusually quiet and she teased me, asking if it was over the gorgeous Greek. When I didn't laugh, she knew something was wrong.

I told her it was worse than she could imagine. I sighed, "I think I'm in love. And he's a musician. And he's twelve years younger than I am. Oh my God, what do I do?"

Yanni's look of love—of course I took the picture.

What I did was follow my heart and begin a romantic adventure that took nine years and spanned four continents.

220

Bless You Jane

WHEN I FIRST realized I was in love, I also realized that since I'd left the show and started living my own life again, I'd managed to put on twenty-five pounds. It was such a joy for me to give up the whole "image thing" that was so important to my career but not to my happiness. After nine years of having to be very professional, I was suddenly free to stay up as late as I wanted, eat anything I felt like cooking, and just be a regular person. Well, that's how I felt until I looked in the mirror and realized I was in love and the heaviest I'd ever been in my life! I was loaded with female insecurity. So now what do I do?

I went on a diet. The only problem was, I'd never been more than five pounds overweight in my life, and I truly had no idea how to be on a diet. So I just stopped eating, but the weight didn't go away. After a few weeks, I called my fitness trainer in LA, Dan Isaacson, and he told me I wasn't losing the weight because when you just stop eating, your metabolism shuts down. So in addition to cutting down on my food intake and eating less rich, high-calorie food, I had to start doing some aerobics. So I hit the store and bought up every Jane Fonda fitness video I could get my hands on. Bless you, Jane.

221

MY FAVORITE SALAD DRESSING

If you're ever on a diet and want something really delicious, this is a killer dressing that you can put on any greens or mixings you like. It's so good you'll swear you're not on a diet.

MAKES A GENEROUS ½ CUP

2½ to 3 tablespoons sherry wine vinegar (or red wine or balsamic)

1 teaspoon Dijon mustard

1 teaspoon heavy cream

¼ cup olive oil

¼ cup vegetable oil

½ teaspoon kosher salt

¼ teaspoon pepper

Whisk ingredients together and serve. Store tightly covered in a jar in the refrigerator for up to a week, shaking vigorously before use.

BABY SPINACH SALAD WITH CITRUS AND AVOCADO

If you're not on a diet and want something really healthy and delicious, this is a great salad.

This light and refreshing salad brings out the best from My Favorite Salad Dressing, with the sherry vinegar highlighting the citrus, and the hint of creaminess echoed in the avocado slices. A sprinkle of toasted walnuts rounds out the flavors nicely, but you can make this salad more of a meal by shaving on some good Parmesan and crumbling some crispy bacon over the top.

½ cup coarsely chopped walnuts

1 pink grapefruit (I like Ruby Red)

1 large navel orange

1 ripe Hass avocado

6 cups baby spinach (or mixed greens)

1 recipe My Favorite Salad Dressing (page 222)

In a dry skillet over medium-high heat, toss the walnut pieces just until they smell fragrant and toasty, 1 to 2 minutes. Pour into a small bowl and set aside. (If you leave them in the hot skillet, they may scorch.)

Trim the orange and grapefruit into membrane-free segments (chefs call these "suprêmes") by this method: working with a sharp knife on a cutting board, cut off the top and bottom of the rind, including any of the white pith beneath. Set the fruit level on the board and slice off the rind and pith in sections. Then hold the fruit in your hand and use a paring knife to cut each segment free of the membrane and dropping the fruit into a bowl, turning the membrane over like the pages of a book.

Halve the avocado and cut thin slices into the citrus bowl. Toss very, very gently just to coat the avocado slices with citrus, to keep them from browning.

Divide the greens among four serving plates and top with the citrus and avocado slices. Drizzle the dressing over the tops of the salads and sprinkle with the toasted walnuts. Serve at once.

Living and Loving in the Moment

THE FIRST TIME Yanni came to visit me at Villa Madera, I was still so taken with him, l could hardly breathe every time I looked at him. I wondered how it was possible to feel so much about someone I hardly knew.

Happy at last.

We spent almost all our days on my boat, out on the beautiful private lake behind the villa.

Courtesy Linda Evans

Sunset on my lake.

We talked endlessly and effortlessly about our lives. In the beginning I would plan wonderful meals for us in the evenings, but I ended up throwing the schedules out because this beautiful Greek man I was falling in love with "lived in the moment." Often the conversation was so compelling, we would stay on the boat until 10 at night. Food wasn't really important for the longest time in our relationship. We were filled with each other.

A Family Affair

SOME OF THE greatest times Yanni and I shared were with his family in Kalamata, Greece. Yanni's mother, Felitsa, was a happy, loving, beautiful soul, who nurtured everyone with her caring nature and her extraordinary cooking. She was the most amazing mom and loving wife I've ever met. I also adore Yanni's dad, Sotiri. A retired banker, Sotiri is incredibly ethical and wise. When we first met, Sortiri was in his seventies and in better shape than me. Yanni's sister, Anda, and I hit it off immediately, and have remained good friends to this day.

Yanni's beautiful parents.

It was an incredibly joyous time. During the day, we'd go off in the boat to a nearby cove to have lunch. Sometimes on the way, dolphins would follow us and leap around the boat. Later we'd swim, play backgammon, and drink ouzo.

Family dinners on the terrace overlooking the sea as the sun set were a nightly ritual. Preparing these incredible feasts was also a family affair. Every year Sotiri would select grapes for his family's "special wine," which when it was ready, would be delivered in a huge barrel that they stored. Sometimes Yanni's beloved grandmother, Anna, would also be in the kitchen helping. Sotiri would bake the bread while Felitsa cooked the best Greek meals I have ever tasted. It was so much fun with everyone helping to bring the feast to the table. They even had Kalamata olives from their own trees, which Uncle Yanni makes and still sends me every year.

Someone's in the kitchen with Felitsa, Yanni's mom.

It seemed everyone in Yanni's family had a special talent with food. Each year, during the month Yanni and I would be with the family, we'd easily gain fifteen pounds each. But believe me, it was worth every ounce.

FELITSA'S APPETIZER MEATBALLS

The addition of mint makes these unique—everyone loves them.

MAKES 5 DOZEN (1-INCH) MEATBALLS
---

1 pound lean ground beef

2 eggs

2 teaspoons minced garlic

¼ cup minced onion

1½ tablespoons minced fresh mint

½ teaspoon dried whole oregano

1 teaspoon kosher salt

1 tablespoon red wine vinegar

4 small slices whole wheat sandwich bread (crust removed)

Vegetable oil for frying

In a large bowl combine the ground beef with the next seven ingredients and blend well.

Put the bread in warm water to soak until soft, then squeeze out excess liquid and squish into a smooth paste. Use your hands to knead the bread with the hamburger mixture, until the bread is incorporated and no longer visible.

Roll mixture into 1-inch balls and fry in a small amount of oil until brown.

An Angel among Us

YANNI INVITED JZ to Greece one summer and the family quickly fell in love with her—as do most people when they meet her. She was only there for a short time, but her stay was memorable. That summer I experienced JZ's generosity and saw how she changed people's lives.

Yanni's family had two women that came daily to help clean during the summer. One was a sweet young girl named Roula; the other was an older woman named Voula. JZ and I always looked forward to seeing them and really enjoyed spending time with them.

We learned from Felitsa that every evening Voula worked at her own very small restaurant up in the mountains. One night we all jumped in the car and drove up to surprise her. We dined outside under the stars and, to our delight, the food was fabulous. After dinner JZ asked if we could see the kitchen. We were amazed when we saw that she had only one small room with a table and a single standing burner on top of it.

The next day JZ went into town and bought Voula the largest professional stove and oven available. If Voula could work her magic on that one burner, imagine what she could now accomplish with this new stove!

JZ also had a profound effect on Roula's life. In the morning, I'd go upstairs to JZ's bedroom and they'd already be deep in conversation about Roula's hopes and dreams. JZ wanted to know what she was going to do now that she had graduated from high school. Roula explained that there weren't many options in the small village where they lived. JZ gave Roula the opportunity of a lifetime: she sent her to America to college. Roula graduated and now works and lives in London. Both these women's lives were changed that summer.

Winter Wonderland

WINTER IS WONDERFUL at Villa Madera. One year Yanni came with his entire family: his mother and father; his older brother, Yorgo, with his wife, Linda, and their two sons; and his younger sister, Anda, with her husband, Richard.

It snowed, which I had rarely experienced and hoped would add to the charm of the Pacific Northwest. Nena and I had planned menus of the most amazing meals I have ever made. I loved this family so much I wanted every meal and moment to be perfect. I had cheeses and wines and specialty foods that I knew they would enjoy flown in from New York and Los Angeles.

Quiet before the storm—the living room at Villa Madera awaits.

In the evenings, the fireplace in the living room (so huge you could walk into it) was the favorite gathering place: ideal for appetizers and a glass of wine. The large living room gave Yorgo and Linda's children lots of room to run and play as we talked by the fire. Yanni's first piano, which we'd brought up to Villa Madera, was waiting in the corner. Perhaps he would play?

A rare snowstorm came in one night and the electricity went out. No ovens, no refrigerator, no heating. My home was an icebox. Fortunately, Villa had fireplaces in most of the rooms, including the bedrooms. Thank God for all the wood we had stored.

My dear, clever Nena had known how to be prepared for times without electricity. She had grown up in a small town outside of Belize without any of the benefits of modern technology. She had encouraged me to buy a small, free-standing two-burner stove, fueled by oil that we purchased the year before. It sat waiting in the garage, as a lifesaver for us.

Bless the Chrysomallis family and their love of adventure and life. Somehow we fed everyone and kept them warm. This visit wasn't as much about the dazzling meals as I had hoped. We all joined together to turn our adversity into intimate conversations by candlelight in front of a roaring fire, with children giggling and running through the dark house. Sometimes the simplest meals are remembered the most.

YORGO AND LINDA'S PESTO

Everyone seems to have their own version of pesto. This one, from Yanni's brother, Yorgo, is my all-time favorite! It has the special addition of a little softened butter, which smooths and rounds out the flavor.

2 tablespoons pine nuts or walnuts

2 cups fresh basil leaves

½ cup olive oil

1 small garlic clove (about 1 teaspoon minced)

¼ teaspoon kosher salt

½ cup grated Parmesan cheese

2 tablespoons grated Romano cheese

3 tablespoons unsalted butter, softened

Place the nuts in a dry skillet over medium-high heat. Toast the nuts, shaking constantly, just until they give off their aroma and are light golden in color, 1 to 2 minutes. Pour them immediately out of the hot skillet and into a dish so they don't burn. Set aside to cool.

In a blender or food processor, put basil leaves, olive oil, garlic, salt, and the cooled nuts. Blend to the desired consistency; some people like a very smooth paste, others prefer a somewhat chunkier texture. At this point, you can freeze the pesto in a covered container for up to four months.

If you're using the pesto right away, add the cheeses and butter and blend until combined. Store in the refrigerator for about one week. To keep it fresh and green, pour ¼ inch of olive oil over the surface, and top it up each time you use the pesto. The oil creates an airtight seal to keep the basil green.

Serve over pasta, chicken, salmon, or whatever your heart desires. I love to mix it with fresh pasta and add lightly salted chopped tomatoes or cubed cooked potatoes and green beans.

Note: If you do decide to freeze it, thaw first and then add the cheeses and butter before serving. To thaw you can use a microwave on low. Be sure never to actually heat the pesto or it will separate.

Sweet Surprises

ONCE IN A while when Yanni wasn't on tour, he'd surprise me and fly up to Washington for a few days. I loved these wonderful unscheduled visits. It was such a sweet surprise.

I wanted to prepare a fabulous dinner for him but he insisted we go out. So I drove him down to a charming Italian restaurant in Tacoma that overlooked the Puget Sound. Anytime Yanni could be by the water he was happy. Dinner was great and hearing about all the wonderful things that were happening in his life was so much better in person than on the phone.

As I pulled up to Villa Madera and pushed the button to open the garage, I slammed my foot on the brake and sat frozen in the car. I was driving a black Jeep SUV that I had brought up from California after I started filming *Dynasty*. As I looked into the garage I saw a black Jeep that looked like a mirror image of my car. I was stunned. How could there be a car in my garage in my spot? And it had a big red bow on it. Under the bow was a big sign that said Yanni Loves Linda. I melted.

I knew Yanni was thinking of getting a brand-new car, his first ever. I remembered how excited he was the past few months when he called to share the different models he had to choose from. Well, he had decided and, as a surprise, he ordered the exact same car for me, fully loaded. He had ordered them directly from the factory and my car was one serial number different from his. It was a beautiful moment for both of us.

The next morning, I made Yanni his favorite breakfast. He nicknamed it "Stand-Up Breakfast" because it was so delicious he wanted to eat it right from the skillet.

Yanni surprised me with a brand-new Jeep. Just because.

STAND-UP BUTTERMILK PANCAKES

Adding a little baking soda to the Bisquick and using buttermilk for the liquid makes a light, crispy, easy-to-make pancake. These delicate cakes taste best with Grade A, real Vermont maple syrup, which has a lighter maple flavor than darker Grade B.

MAKES 14 (4-INCH) PANCAKES

---

1 cup Bisquick

¼ teaspoon baking soda

1½ cups buttermilk

1 teaspoon melted unsalted butter, plus additional for serving

4 egg whites

7 tablespoons vegetable oil
8 tablespoons (1 stick) unsalted butter, clarified (see Note below)
Pure maple syrup, gently warmed, for serving

Blend together Bisquick and baking soda in a mixing bowl, smoothing out lumps with a fork. Add the buttermilk and 1 teaspoon of melted butter and mix on low with an electric mixer.

In another mixing bowl, beat the egg whites until soft peaks are formed. Take half of the beaten egg whites and fold into the Bisquick mixture, mixing well by hand with a rubber spatula, then fold in the remaining half, again by hand with a spatula.

Put 1 tablespoon of oil and 1 tablespoon of clarified butter in a 10-inch frying pan over medium-low heat. When the oil is heated, pour ¼ cup of the pancake mixture in the frying pan, and cook the pancake until edges are light and crispy brown. Cook only two pancakes in the oil and butter in the pan, then add another 1 tablespoon of oil and 1 tablespoon of clarified butter, and continue cooking. (The amount of oil/butter you will need will change depending on the size of the frying pan and the number of pancakes you cook. You will need enough oil/butter mixture to make them crispy.)

Serve immediately, or they will lose their lightness and crispiness, with a little melted butter and warmed maple syrup on top.

Note: To make clarified butter, melt the butter slowly. Let it sit for a bit to separate. Skim off the foam that rises to the top, and gently pour the butter off the milk solids, which have settled to the bottom. One stick (8 tablespoons) of butter will produce about 7 tablespoons of clarified butter.

A Symphony of Sights and Sounds

MY LIFE WITH Yanni was a whirlwind. It was at the peak of my career and Yanni's was taking off like a rocket. Ironically, I had left *Dynasty* because I craved privacy. So what did I do? I fell in love with an up-and-coming star. But I was genuinely thrilled for him because I knew it was his dream and his time.

For nine years, Yanni and I traveled the world together, often for his concerts. From the Forbidden City to the Acropolis, it was a very exciting and romantic time in my life. I'll never forget being taken on a private tour at sunrise of the Taj Mahal, which was built as one of the greatest monuments to love.

Yanni's Other Girl; or, My Rival in Venice

BETWEEN TOURING, YANNI and I took a little time for ourselves in Italy, staying at the Hotel Cipriani on Giudecca Island, a short boat ride from Piazza San Marco in Venice.

Our room had a charming balcony, overlooking the water and Venice across the way. The day we arrived, we were sitting outside when Yanni was suddenly enchanted by the most beautiful song. It was coming from a sweet little bird that had landed on a nearby tree. Yanni has perfect pitch, so he was able to replicate the bird's song. Soon, the two were serenading one another; it was a truly magical moment.

What was really amazing is that this was not a one-time affair: every morning, coffee in hand, Yanni went out on the balcony to rendezvous with his Italian girlfriend, and the two would make beautiful music together. I would have been jealous if I wasn't enjoying it so much.

When it was finally time to leave, Yanni went out to say good-bye, but sadly, for the first time, she wasn't there. I could tell Yanni was really disappointed, as was I. But we had a plane to catch, so we couldn't wait around any longer, and hurried down to the dock to take the launch back to Venice.

As we were boarding the motorboat, I could see him stalling, looking around, still hoping. Then, suddenly we heard her sweet song. His little bird was perched on a branch, singing her good-bye. I wasn't the only one with tears in my eyes.

When he returned home to the States, Yanni composed a song using her melody and then he performed it for the first time at his concert in

China's Forbidden City. The song, which he named "Nightingale," always touches my heart, as does the memory of them in Venice.

ROASTED PEPPER AND MOZZARELLA SALAD WITH VINAIGRETTE

I love things that I can make ahead and don't have to assemble until the last minute. This salad is elegant and quick—the only thing that takes time is roasting and peeling the peppers. I like to use peppers in different colors: look for red, orange, and yellow.

MAKES 6 SERVINGS

3 bell peppers

6 tablespoons extra-virgin olive oil

2½ tablespoons red wine vinegar

⅛ teaspoon garlic clove, minced

2 teaspoons or more to taste anchovy paste

1 pound tomatoes, matching the size with the mozzarella balls

3 (4-ounce) balls fresh mozzarella, sliced ¼-inch thick or 6 (2-ounce) balls

Fresh basil leaves, to taste

12 kalamata olives

Place the peppers on a baking sheet and broil until the tops become charred. Turn and continue charring until they are slightly blackened all over. Remove from the broiler and wrap in a damp towel (or close them in a paper bag) until cooled.

When cool, peel the peppers and cut in two, lengthwise. Core and seed the peppers, and then cut them in half again so that each pepper makes four large slices. Place the peppers in a shallow glass dish.

Combine the olive oil, vinegar, garlic, and anchovy paste to make the dressing. After mixing the dressing extremely well with a wire whisk, pour half over the peppers, allowing the peppers to marinate for 6 to 8 hours. After marinating, remove the peppers and arrange two slices each on individual plates.

Remove the core from the tomatoes and cut a thin slice off the opposite end; discard. Then slice the tomatoes into ¼-inch-thick slices and arrange on the plates, alternating between the peppers (two slices per plate).

Next, drain the mozzarella cheese and pat dry with paper towels. Cut the mozzarella into ¼-inch-thick slices. Place one slice on each tomato slice.

Julienne the basil leaves into thin, ⅛-inch-thick ribbons. Scatter the cut basil leaves on top of each tomato/mozzarella combination, to taste.

Add salt and pepper to taste to the arrangement, then drizzle some of the remaining dressing on top. Garnish with two olives per plate and serve at room temperature.

Finding My Voice

I HAD RECEIVED a wonderful invitation to speak in front of hundreds of women at a convention in Anaheim, California. Greeny insisted it was a great opportunity and that I should do it in spite of my terror. I can't even count the number of times Bunky has had to drag me out from under the covers on my bed to accept an award that was given to me for *Dynasty*. "Get up" she'd say. "You have to do this!" And she'd push me to the mirror to get myself together. I had been working at RSE on a discipline to help me overcome my fear of public speaking and I decided to accept the invitation. Maybe some of the work I had been doing was starting to sink in, I tried to convince myself.

I flew down to LA a few days early to be with Yanni. I loved staying with him in his house in Laurel Canyon. We mostly ordered takeout so we could have more time to sit together and talk. Bacon-wrapped shrimp with pesto and a crispy cheese pizza in a wood-fired oven— perfect every time. I was having such a great time with Yanni that the nervous thing I usually had proceeding a public appearance wasn't there. "Oh," I thought, "Love makes everything better!"

Mike and Bunky picked me up midmorning. I could sense her watching me to see how I was doing. In typical Bunky fashion, she made me laugh all the way there.

As I was about to go onstage, I was surprised how calm I felt. They introduced me and I began talking about my life and the lessons I've learned, the insecurities and doubts that we all have as women, despite how successful we are or appear to be.

Halfway through my speech I was in the zone. You would need a hook to get me off the stage. I was loving it.

Then, in a flash of light, I saw myself in a discipline at RSE where I had left behind my past and reinvented myself to be able to do what I was now doing.

I was so overwhelmed with joy, I started to cry. I realized in that moment that nothing is carved in stone. Attitudes, painful memories, it could all be given up in a moment. I was in awe of the potential of the mind. Of course, the audience had no idea what I was going through or why I was suddenly smiling and crying, but when I explained how I'd just overcome my fear of public speaking, they burst into applause.

That day I started my public speaking career. It's now one of the most rewarding things I do.

Always a Song in My Heart

MY RELATIONSHIP WITH Yanni opened doors to the world of music that I would never have entered. I was privileged to witness his entire creative process, from watching him compose his music, to recording for months in the studio, and, finally, to performing before live audiences around the world. What a magical ride. No matter how many performances I sat through, year after year, I was spellbound.

His music seemed to bridge all ages. The young and the old were on their feet applauding every night. Everyone, including me, left the theater uplifted.

I watched this beautiful, creative man also take on the business end of producing his concerts, an enormous task when it came to performing his music in Greece at the Acropolis, India at the Taj Mahal, and China in the Forbidden City.

No relationship ends without some warnings, and again, like most people, I tried my best to ignore them for as long as I could. Yanni was consumed with making his concerts unforgettable. I knew when I met him that his music would come first. It was a mistress I could live with.

But as time went on, it became his music along with performing, promoting, and producing. He was exhausted and stretched to the limit. I'd always admired his ability to work endlessly for something he loved and was passionate about. After nine years, somehow our relationship got lost in the journey. But I wouldn't have missed what we shared together for the world.

As American as Apple Pie, Almost

ONE OF THE times my stepdaughter Sean had flown in from LA to visit me at Villa Madera, I decided to make us a special dinner (for once she wasn't on a diet). I wanted to surprise her and make her favorite dessert: apple pie.

Villa Madera had an elegant formal dining room, but I loved having dinners in the library, with its rich dark wood paneling and shelves filled with handcrafted leather-bound books. For these more intimate dinners, I found a small round table that fit perfectly in front of the fireplace.

Once I'd selected a menu of some of her favorite dishes, I decided to try a new apple cider pie recipe that I had recently discovered that sounded outrageously delicious. Since Sean and I were visiting, I asked Nena to make the pie for us.

We shared a wonderful meal and then Nena came in with a big smile on her face carrying her beautiful, picture-perfect pie. She cut Sean a big piece and stepped back to proudly watch her take the first bite. And as she did, Sean's eyes squinted and her face scrunched up like a prune. Then she turned away to spit (as politely as possible) into her napkin.

Nena and I stared at her in shock. I didn't understand how she couldn't love it. "Taste it!" Sean said. I did and instantly I was puckering and squinting, too, but I now knew why. Nena had used apple cider vinegar instead of apple cider. If that wasn't enough, the recipe called for boiling down cups of cider into a syrupy consistency, which made the vinegar flavor and punch even more intense. It turns out Nena had never heard of apple cider, only apple cider vinegar.

We all started laughing, because the joke was that Sean was still on a diet, since the pretty pie was inedible.

Nena, making her magic.

BEST EVER APPLE PIE

Here's the recipe!

MAKES 1 (10-INCH) DEEP-DISH PIE (USING A 10- X 2-INCH PIE PLATE)

FOR CRUST:

2½ cups all-purpose flour

1 teaspoon kosher salt

1 teaspoon sugar

4 ounces (1 stick) unsalted butter, chilled and cut into pieces

4 ounces (½ cup) butter-flavored shortening, chilled

5 to 6 tablespoons ice water

FOR FILLING:

2⅔ cups apple cider

2½ pounds (7 to 8) Granny Smith apples, peeled, cored, and sliced

¾ pound (2 to 3) Golden Delicious apples, peeled, cored, and sliced

1 cup sugar

¼ cup all-purpose flour

¾ teaspoon ground cinnamon

¼ teaspoon salt

¼ teaspoon ground mace

1 tablespoon freshly squeezed lemon juice

3 tablespoons unsalted butter, cut into small pieces

FOR THE CRUST:

Combine the flour, salt, and sugar in a food processor. Add butter and shortening and pulse until mixture forms coarse crumbs. Add 2 tablespoons of ice water to the flour mixture. With the machine running, add additional water a tablespoon at a time until clumps form. Mold the dough into two balls, shape into two disks, and wrap in plastic wrap. Refrigerate for 30 minutes.

FOR THE FILLING:

Bring the apple cider to a boil in a saucepan over medium-high heat for about 20 minutes, until reduced to about ⅔ cup.

In a large bowl, combine the apples, sugar, flour, cinnamon, salt, and mace. Add reduced cider and lemon juice. Toss well.

FOR THE PIE ASSEMBLY:

Preheat oven to 425°F.

On a lightly floured surface, roll out one disk of dough into a 14-inch-diameter circle. Transfer to a 10-inch pie plate. Don't trim the edges yet. Turn the apples into the crust, and dot with the butter pieces.

On a lightly floured surface, roll out the remaining dough into a 13-inch round. Roll it up on the rolling pin and unroll it on top of the pie. Trim the edges, leaving a 1-inch rim of dough. Fold that under and crimp the edges with your fingers or a fork. Slit the top crust with a knife a few times to let the steam escape.

Put the pie in the oven, with a baking sheet on the rack below it to catch any drips. Bake 30 minutes, then reduce oven temperature to 350°F. Continue baking 45 minutes more. Cover the rim of the crust with foil if it darkens too quickly.

Remove the pie from the oven and allow it to cool at least 1 hour before cutting.

Animal Lovers Unite

JOHN FORSYTHE WAS always riding high when he would come to work after a weekend with his racehorses. Horses were his passion. His dream was to have a home where he could look out the window and see them grazing. Happily, after *Dynasty*, his dream came true. John lived on a magnificent thoroughbred farm in California's beautiful Santa Inez Valley.

Because of John's love of breeding and racing horses, he met and became friends with Marjorie Lindheimer Everett. Marje and I met in the mid-80s, and I have come to love her dearly. She and Bunky are the only people I call every day.

Marje is a woman ahead of her time. She was the owner and CEO of the famous Hollywood Park racetrack. She reminds me a lot of Barbara Stanwyck, in that she puts up a tough front to hide a gentle heart.

Marje is a powerful woman who accomplished greatness in what was still very much "a man's world," doing jobs in the 1940s like scouting players for her father's football team, the Los Angeles Dons. Then later, after her father died in the 1960s, she took over his racetrack in Chicago.

I often stay with her when I come to LA because she is such an inspiration to me. At nearly ninety, she can hold me spellbound recalling the stories of her remarkable life.

In addition to our love of animals, another thing Marje and I definitely have in common is that we love bringing people together to celebrate over good food. She continues to be famous for her parties, not just because of the amazing cuisine and ambiance she provides, but because she unites friends from all walks of life, making for memorable evenings.

My friendship with Marje has enriched my life in countless ways. One year I flew with her to Texas for the Breeders' Cup. As we walked around the racetrack, it was beautiful to see how many lives she's touched. There was an endless sea of people coming up to thank her for the opportunities she gave them and the difference it made in their lives.

Aaron Spelling—the man that changed my life.

A few years later, Marje gave me an unforgettable opportunity.

When I had heard that Aaron Spelling was seriously ill, I sent him a note telling him how grateful I was that he chose me for the part of Krystle. He sent me back the dearest letter that I treasure to this day. As time went by, I shared with Marje that I was sad that I couldn't see Aaron and tell him in person.

She had been best friends with the Spellings for years. Unbeknownst to me, she called Candy, and in spite of the fact that Aaron had not been going out at all, she arranged for them to come to her house for an intimate dinner. She also invited John Forsythe. We had the most beautiful evening, reminiscing and laughing about all the great times we spent together. It was wonderful to be able to personally share with him the difference he made in my life.

The evening was bittersweet, because we all knew it would be the last time we'd ever see each other. It is a memory that I will always cherish.

Leap of Faith

OVER THE YEARS, every so often, I'd receive offers to do plays. But since I'd never even considered doing theater, Greeny stopped bothering to ask if I was interested. He would just turn down any offers. So I would never even have heard of a play called *Legends* if it weren't for my friend Nolan Miller, who asked me to read it.

After I finished it, I remember thinking, I love this play! I think I'm going to do it. The premise was empowering: two strong women who hate each other, but because of circumstances, they end up friends, united in a common goal. I felt the play was a wonderful metaphor for life: even our enemies can help us reach mutually beneficial places.

Another thing I loved about the play is that it spoke to women, affirming that we may be in our sixties and seventies, but we still have plenty of life left in us; there are still things to do, to make known, and to conquer.

Also, because I felt I'd overcome my stage fright, thanks to all the speaking engagements I'd been doing around the world, I knew the crowds themselves wouldn't be a problem. What I didn't foresee was the difference between speaking and performing, particularly in an arena I knew so little about: the stage.

Everyone assured me the transition from film to stage would be a breeze. Especially since the part of Leatrice (originally played in the 1980s by Mary Martin) wasn't all that different from Krystle, my character on *Dynasty*. The same was true about my costar's role, Sylvia (originally played by Carol Channing)—it was very similar to Alexis Carrington, and would be played by Joan Collins.

The day I arrived in New York to start rehearsing, I knew I was in for a bumpy ride. I realized how much I had to learn and how fast I had to learn it before facing thousands of people. I was so out of my element, I

250

Here we go again.

251

didn't even have a good sense of the basics: stage right, upstage, down-stage. What I really wanted to do was exit stage left and keep running, but I kept telling myself I was too professional to do that.

After a few days, I knew I needed some extra help, so I started going to a coach right after a full day of rehearsals. I'd catch a cab and go straight to her studio where we'd work until two or three in the morning. The routine was exhausting, but well worth it. I was getting a crash course in stage acting, literally days before we would start performing for an audi-ence. As we began the tour in Toronto, I just kept plowing through the obstacles, holding to my belief that there is always a gift in every problem.

My first gift was the theater experience itself. I'd always heard it was incredibly rewarding, but I couldn't really relate until I was a part of it. There is something so satisfying about working in front of an audience. It's a living connection; you and the audience are one.

Making new friends was another gift that was easy to recognize. Joan and I were working with an amazing cast of talented and support-ive actors I still keep in touch with. The play also gave me the opportu-nity to get even closer to Bunky's daughter Tracy whom I'd known since she was just a little thing and has always been like a member of my fam-ily. Bunky knew that she wasn't up to spending nine months touring the States, but she wanted to be absolutely certain I was well taken care of, so she asked Tracy if she would take over for her. Lucky for me, Tracy thought it sounded like a wonderful adventure.

A mother of three grown gorgeous girls of her own, Tracy is a chip off the old Bunky block. She has an outrageous sense of humor and, just like her mom, could always find a way to make me laugh no matter what kind of stress we were under.

Tracy just slipped effortlessly right into Bunky's shoes, which was a lifesaver for me, with all the unknowns and the resulting pressures. She was forever thinking up new ways to keep me light and laughing, in-cluding getting a fart machine to shock visitors that were obviously expecting to meet a very different Linda Evans from the one with the outrageous noises echoing out of her dressing room.

Eating My Way across the Country

ANOTHER ENDEARING ASPECT of touring the United States was that in every new city we played, we tried to find time to visit the most popular spots. Sometimes it was museums, or a historical district, or my favorite: famous restaurants. I ate well, gained weight, and savored every minute of it.

By the end of *Legends'* nine-month run, despite all the challenges, I was sad that it was going to be over: I actually loved doing the play. I was very touched that the director, John Bowab, and the producer, Ben Sprecher, thanked me and said that they would love to work with me again.

I still have the gift that the director gave me on opening night, a beautiful hand-painted blue box with an inspiring inscription from Henry David Thoreau: "I have learned . . . that if one advances confidently in the direction of his dreams, and endeavors to live the life which he has imagined, he will meet with a success unexpected in common hours."

Legends taught me many lessons and gave me great gifts, some surprising, many empowering. In the end, I could be proud of my performance on- and offstage.

BANANA, LEMONGRASS, AND COCONUT SOUP

When the play came to LA, I was fortunate enough to stay at one of my favorite hotels, the Four Seasons. I had the best soup there I'd ever tasted. I was so excited that I just had to have the recipe. The Four Seasons' executive chef, Ashley James, was kind enough to give it to me. I hope you love it as much as I do.

MAKES ABOUT 5 CUPS, FOR 8–10 APPETIZER SERVINGS

---

4 tablespoons olive oil

1 cup diced onion

½ cup diced celery

½ cup diced carrot

2 teaspoons chopped garlic

2 teaspoons ground cumin

1 teaspoon Sambal chili paste

1 bunch cilantro, finely chopped

3 whole very ripe organic bananas, sliced

1 cup fresh orange juice

4 cups chicken stock

4 sticks of split lemongrass

Salt and white pepper to taste

2 cups coconut milk

Heat the oil in a thick-bottomed saucepot over medium-high heat.

Add onion, celery, and carrot; cook until the vegetables are nicely caramelized, add the chopped garlic, toasted cumin, Sambal, chopped cilantro, and then the sliced bananas, cook for a further 2 minutes until the bananas become mushy.

Deglaze the saucepot with the fresh orange juice stirring well, and scraping the bottom of the pot to remove all the flavors. Let the juice reduce by half. Stir in the chicken stock. Tie the split lemongrass with a piece of cotton kitchen string to make a small bundle, and add it with salt and pepper. Simmer and cook 20 minutes.

Remove the lemongrass, then puree all ingredients together with an immersion blender, or food processor. Strain the soup into a clean saucepot, pressing it through a sieve with the back of a spoon. Stir in the coconut cream and bring the soup to a boil. Adjust seasoning if necessary by adding more salt and pepper.

Serve in a cappuccino cup.

From the Frying Pan into the Fire

AFTER THE PLAY, I returned home to a number of stressful situations. Bunky was struggling with macular degeneration and heart issues. Part of me couldn't come to terms with the fact that I couldn't *fix* her. My sister Kat was battling cancer (which thank God she beat) but while she was going through it, I felt a helpless desperation for her. It was incredibly hard to see anyone I loved suffering. On top of that, some of my professional and personal relationships had become strained.

It was one thing after another, and things were spinning out of control. My control. I was on an emotional roller coaster that sent my blood pressure up over 200. I'd been remarkably healthy all of my life, so this news further unnerved me. I was put on medication, which made me disoriented. So I decided to take myself off it. Unfortunately, that only made things worse. One day I was simply trying to pick up one of my cats when I blacked out and fell on my face.

At this point I really wasn't sure how to put myself back together. It was completely against my nature to take any prescription medication, but I knew I needed help. I reluctantly took what the doctors gave me, which meant one pill led to another, then to another, and soon my stomach went out, then I couldn't do this, and I couldn't do that. . . .

The whole fabric of my reality frayed. For the first time in my life, I found myself battling against depression. I fought back. My faith and the knowledge I had from years of studying mind, body, and spiritual connections helped me. And I *would* start to feel better. Until something else would happen and knock me back down. Like when my sister Charlie suddenly needed surgery.

In my heart I knew the drugs were not going to help because I wasn't fixing what needed fixing. I was just treating a symptom. I was putting a Band-Aid over a problem that wasn't even close to healing. I didn't know how to fix so many problems all at once. I didn't know how to protect everyone. I didn't know how to be happy unless everyone I cared about was happy.

Finally, I decided I needed to get off everything, so I went to a facility in Northern California that puts you on a doctor-supervised water fast. Within a few days I could tell I'd made the right decision; I was getting some of my clarity back, my life back. It was a healing time for me. I had stepped away from everyone else's lives so that I had the time to reflect on what I needed to change in mine.

During those twenty-one days, I saw that it was *my perspective* of how life had to be that was making me unhappy. I couldn't change what was happening around me, but I had the power to change how I reacted to it. My suffering wouldn't change theirs. It was a recipe for disaster. I was looking outside myself for the answers, instead of inside. I finally saw that I would have some peace if I just saw things as they were and accepted them.

It was time to take off my rose-colored glasses and see all the colors of life, the sweet and the sad. I now understood that I could survive and hold my own joy, no matter what the people I love might be going through in their lives.

It has been one of my greatest gifts.

Hell's Kitchen:
Heaven on Earth for Me

HELL'S KITCHEN WAS really heaven to me. In retrospect, I see how outrageous my decision was to fly to London to do a cooking show I knew nothing about. Somehow I couldn't say no, so I knew it was going to be an unforgettable ride. How exciting that at sixty-six I was doing things I never would have taken on when I was younger!

Long before the invitation to do *Hell's Kitchen*, I had read an article in one of my food magazines about Marco Pierre White and was fascinated by his life. He was the youngest English chef to ever receive three Michelin stars. When he reached the pinnacle of his success he walked away from it all for the next seven years.

When I learned that Marco was coming back to do *Hell's Kitchen*, I was thrilled. Over the years, I'd paid a lot of money to take cooking lessons, and now they were offering to fly me to London (a city I love), and not only was Marco going to teach us, but three other world-class chefs as well: Mario Batali, Raymond Blanc, and Jean-Christophe Novelli.

With all my heart, I wanted to do it, although I didn't really understand what it would entail, since I haven't watched a lot of reality television. Plus, this was a British production, which I knew even less about. I just knew that I wanted the experience.

They had booked me at my favorite hotel in London, The Dorchester, so I just assumed that I would go in to work every day, then return each night to the hotel—not torture by anyone's standards.

Shortly before I was scheduled to leave, we learned that I'd actually only be staying one night at The Dorchester. After that, I'd be living on the set, literally locked in with the other eight celebrity contestants for at least the first week. Beyond that, it would depend on whether the chef "sacked" you or, if by some miracle, you made it to the second week.

We also learned that we wouldn't be able to communicate with anyone on the outside: no visitors, cell phones, TV, books, magazines. Just cooking 24–7.

So, off I went to begin life in *Hell's Kitchen*, and, God, am I glad I did. It was more wonderful than I could have ever imagined, despite the fact that it was a reality show designed to create as much drama among all the contestants as possible. Having just come off so much real-life drama of my own, my goal was to experience as much joy and fun as I could, while doing what I love.

It turned out that I was the only American in this wonderful assortment of amazing talents, including a famous soccer player, a rapper, a model, a talk show host, a businessman, an actor, and a comedian.

Courtesy of ITV/Rex Features

My family in Hell. *Left to right: Anthea Turner, Grant Bovey, Danielle Bux, me, Adrian Edmondson, Jody Latham, Niomi McLean-Daley, Bruce Grobbelaar, Marco Pierre White.*

The first night, the eight of us had dinner while they began filming us, and I decided to see if anyone else was in the mood to just have fun. I was delighted that everyone felt the same way. Of course, there did end up being some drama. It was impossible to avoid. Also, this wasn't a set for a cooking school. They had built an actual restaurant, which each night would fill up with people, some famous, all expecting a meal prepared by a three-star Michelin chef and his staff, comprised primarily of the eight of us. But for the most part, we all really did get along incredibly well and we were all genuinely sad when one person had to be sent home by Marco or got voted off by the viewing audience.

We were building friendships and really starting to care for one another. Whenever I'd have trouble, because of the language barrier (don't laugh—the combination of slang or heavy accents left me completely confused), everyone would laugh, but someone would always step in and help. If one of us failed at our cooking assignment, another covered as best we could for them. Finding myself with these terrific, caring people was a blessing. Each of them was a treasure. On top of all that, I was learning so much about cooking and the passion and dedication it takes to be a great chef.

We had been living cooking, night and day, for over a week when they asked us to catch an eel with our bare hands out of a tank on the set and bring it into the kitchen area in a net. I knew the minute they gave us the challenge what they were going to ask us to do. Sure enough, as we entered the kitchens, we could see areas with huge meat cleavers set out for us.

Like I've said, I don't even kill spiders. Marco had explained to us during the show the necessity of having reverence for the food we were working with. I love that Native Americans blessed the animals that they killed, and I have always blessed my food before I eat it. Now I was faced with an enormous opportunity.

I knew the eel wasn't going to be put back where they got it just because I refused to kill it. I saw a bigger picture. I saw my hypocrisy about eating meat: I wanted to think of it as mystery food wrapped in plastic at the market. I didn't identify with it or take responsibility for what is required for my eating any living thing. I made the choice to step up for the experience. I blessed the eel and thanked it with all my heart and prayed that I could do it swiftly, so it felt no pain. Everyone was shocked that I did it. But in that moment, I felt an enormous gift come to me: an appreciation and reverence for all that give of their life so that we can have life.

In spite of the number of cooking challenges they gave us during the day, and the growing number of people we served at the restaurant every night, I made up my mind never to let the pressure get to me—not even when Marco was yelling at me. I took it all in stride. I learned from doing *Legends* to take the pressure and turn it into excitement. And it was a blast!

At the end of the evening, I didn't want to go to bed. I was so filled with energy from what we had done, how we had joined together to feed all these people. It was one of the most exhilarating times I've ever had. Then to top it all off, somehow, I managed to make it through the entire two weeks. Why the audience voted for me, I'm not sure, but I know I'm grateful beyond words that I won!

Me and Chef Marco Pierre White, my culinary hero.

HELL'S SALMON

Adrian Edmondson and I were in the final competition together. He's a fabulous comedian, musician, devoted husband, and father, and I love him dearly. He was a big part of my joy every day. I wanted to include a recipe of his in this book. He is an amazing cook, and if I could have voted, it would have been for him. Unfortunately for me, Ade is an instinctive chef, making it hard to pin him down to a recipe with exact measurements. So I am going to share the recipe that I created for the final cooking challenge. Ade won the appetizer and I won the main course with what I lovingly now call Hell's Salmon.

MAKES 6 SERVINGS

¼ cup clarified unsalted butter (see page 29)

6 (6-ounce) skinless salmon fillets, about ¾-inch thick

1 cup seasoned butter, at room temperature (see page 96)

Put the clarified butter into a large nonstick skillet over medium-high heat. After 2 minutes, when the butter is hot, add the salmon fillets. Let them sizzle, without moving them, for 2½ minutes, then flip the fillets carefully and continue to cook for another 3 minutes. Place the salmon on a warmed serving plate.

Remove the pan from the heat. Wipe the pan with a paper towel to remove excess butter. In the still-warm pan, add a ¼ cup of the softened seasoned butter at a time, whisking constantly, until it forms a creamy sauce. If you need a bit more heat, hold the pan *briefly* over very low heat (only for a moment, then remove again), never letting the butter melt completely or the sauce will separate. (This sauce derives its velvetlike smoothness from whisking in the butter so it blends into and thickens the sauce without melting outright.) Put the sauce in a gravy boat, and serve separately.

If you're not a soy sauce lover, you can make this salmon and use Julia Child's Hollandaise sauce (page 80) instead.

My Just Desserts

What you get by reaching your destination
is not nearly as important as what you become
by reaching your destination.

—Zig Ziglar

LIKE A GREAT recipe, we are all unique, seasoned by our life over the years. I may be sixty-eight years old but in many ways I'm just getting started. There is something glorious about getting older as a woman. A freedom from so many of society's agreements, that age helps you to let go of. There's a peace that comes to us when we know what's important and what isn't.

I'm a part of an ever-growing group of beautiful people called the baby boomers. There are 70 million of us and we still have a lot to say and do. The wisdom that we accrue is the gift each of us carries with us. I'm waiting for our society to finally recognize this unseen quality for the treasure that it is in our lives. It's the jewel in our crown, so to speak, when we live a long and aware life.

I'm thrilled that in writing this book, I've finally completed this part of my dream and I'm excited to see what I can cast into my future. I'm not the woman I used to be. I'm rich in experience and looking for new and wonderful adventures to add to this magical gift called life.

Today—looking forward to the future.